The Wisdom of Well-Being

A Mind, Body, Spirit approach to Creating and Maintaining
Optimal Health and Well-Being

Dr. Diana Joy Ostroff,
Naturopathic Physician and Doctor of
Traditional Asian Medicine and Acupuncture

Dr. Diana Joy Ostroff is proud to celebrate her 22st year of dedicated healing and personalized care as a Nationally Certified Naturopathic Physician and Acupuncturist. Since founding the Center for Natural Healing in Honolulu, Hawaii, she has specialized in Primary Family Health Care, comprehensive Women's Health issues, Holistic Pediatrics, Nutritional support, Detoxification, and Life-Coaching. She has treated a wide range of individuals who have suffered with chronic and life challenging illness, addiction, and injury and has been witness to their marvelous and often miraculous recoveries. I am continually gratified and elated by the overwhelmingly positive natural healing experiences of my patients. In recovery, their personal achievements in overcoming acute and chronic health conditions, personal, lifestyle and conception issues, as well as formerly resistant debilitating diseases are profound. The success stories I hear from my patients day in and day out have given me a life filled with devotion to my work and a deep gratitude for the gift that I have been blessed with, to bring healing to the planet, naturally; one person at a time.

–Dr. Diana Joy Ostroff: Dr. Ostroff is a well known and frequently requested public speaker, often presenting her "Wisdom of Well-Being" natural health seminars to large audiences in Hawaii.

The Wisdom of Well-being

TABLE OF CONTENTS

DEDICATION AND ACKNOWLEDGEMENTS

I am so thrilled and excited to finally have gotten this long overdue book written and put together and I would like to express my extreme gratitude to all of the wonderful individuals who assisted and supported me through its production.

First and foremost, I thank God for blessing me with so many gifts and seeing me through all the trials and tribulations that it took me to get to this place of such great overflowing abundance in spirit and inspiration, that I could no longer keep it inside.

My father, who, despite his hardship, fear and pain supported me through all of my 14 years of higher education; while doing his best to be a loving role model. My sister, Linda, who always inspired me to follow a path of unique individuality and helped me to believe in myself with her encouragement and praise, as well as giving critical feedback enabling me to reflect and grow. My brother Dirk, for his consistency and stability in handling the mundane. My biggest fan, best friend and business associate, Richard Baccigaluppi who stood by me through the hard times, was always there for me to assist with any project, or to just get me out of the office; and who believes in me enough to go out on a limb with support in any way that he can.

My assistant, Rhonda Grimmer Waldinger who knows how to manage my office, children and staff and has been there as a loving and supportive friend.

My children, Solomon and Aaron, who give me a reason to work so hard and teach me how to be a whole, real and sensitive loving mother. And to Tom Magee, their father who always knows how to make me laugh under any circumstance and has been encouraging me to write this book all along.

And to my amazing PLD mastermind 309 team, who assisted me in raising the bar with empowering inspiration and loving support. To my patients, who over the last 20 years have trusted me to care for them in a way that demonstrated my belief in their ability to create vital health through perseverance, discipline, and self-love.

FORWARD

For twenty-two years now, I have been practicing as a licensed Naturopathic Doctor (N.D.), twelve years ago receiving my Doctor of Oriental Medicine and Acupuncture National License. I have had the honor of treating thousands of patients and their families to alter the course of their lives and bring them back on track with their body's inherent self-healing capabilities.

I have learned that "doctors don't heal, and drugs don't heal." Rather, nature heals and the body heals itself when treated properly. It can be guided gently toward what is inherently healing, balancing, and in harmony with nature. The body contains self-healing, self-repairing, self-recuperating properties that will restore health when given the correct nutrition, guidance, and instruction. When I was 31 years old, I was diagnosed with a "fatal" disease. I had applied for a life insurance policy and had to go in for a physical exam. When the tests came back, my liver enzymes were at a life-threatening level of over 2000. I was told that I was going to die within weeks. I attributed this issue to stress and a variety of over-indulgences beginning in my teens, growing up on the east coast. It continued all the way through medical school where I burned the candle on both ends, meeting the demands of school. I had over-consumed caffeine and sugar as a coping mechanism and was certain that it would catch up with me and "It" certainly did.

While face-to-face with the person who was sharing this situation with me, I soberly decided at the time of that diagnosis, that I would see him again with a big smile on my face when I was all better. I was resolved that this was indeed my opportunity to heal myself and that when I did, I would be in a much better situation to assist my patients in healing themselves.

"Physician heal thyself." I knew that this was indeed my ultimate test. I was determined to restore my health to one hundred percent. It took extreme dedication and practices that I will describe for you in my book, and I am thrilled to say that it worked. I became one hundred percent, healthier than I had EVER been in my life, and that optimal health has remained with me.

I went on to have my two children in my forties through natural childbirth. Today, I am a happy, healthy mother and esteemed doctor in the community assisting other mothers, children, and men in finding their true happiness and wholeness through an integrated life-style while attending to their mental, emotional, physical and spiritual well¬being.

I am clear that my role as doctor/healer is to be able to walk my talk and be a radiant example of what is possible for my patients who put their faith and trust in me. The original meaning of the word "doctor" in Latin is teacher. I strive to be that person every day, in my work and in my life.

There have been an estimated 100,000 reported deaths in the U.S. each year, caused iatrogenically (as the result of the use or misuse of prescription medicine). This number does not account for the millions of naive individuals who suffer in silence, never considering that their pains and problems have any relationship to the drugs that have been prescribed to them by their medical doctors.

How often I hear stories of how one medication has been prescribed to a patient to alleviate the symptoms caused by the use of another medication. In the last ten years, there has also been an alarming increase in cancer rates in children between 1 and 14 years old in the United States. There had never been incidences of this prevalence before.

I am told by desperate mothers wishing for a cure for their sick child that their innocent baby has been on antibiotics, prednisone, steroid creams, and inhalers from birth, for symptoms that I view as easily treatable without the need for any chemical drugs. These mothers, desperate to see their babies well, give their infants whatever their pediatrician prescribes. They do not realize that the pills, creams, and sprays containing chemical toxins and pharmacological agents are causing more serious harm than good. The drugs perpetuate a decline in the child's immune system that could have been prevented and the symptoms alleviated by the careful attention and application of a natural cure.

So often there is a simple cure requiring a physician trained as a naturopathic doctor. The Naturopath can recognize the initial cause of the disease and treat that, rather than masking the symptoms with a variety of harsh, detrimental chemicals which upset the delicate balance of every cell in the human body, while inhibiting the immune system's inherent wisdom to heal itself. An example of this model was a young couple who brought their 18 month-old baby into see me for a second opinion. Their gastroenterologist had recommended that the constipated infant go in for a surgical procedure requiring the removal of the blocked portion of the intestines. This would entail general anesthesia, antibiotics, pain relieving formulas, as well as a barium enema before the surgery and stool softeners afterwards.

I recommended a simple change in diet, an increase in water intake, did some gentle abdominal manipulations and recommended a micro-flora and herbal combination that was compatible with the infants constitution. In two days, the infant was having normal bowel movements and was able to avoid this invasive procedure.

I entered into this field of Naturopathic Medicine due to my inherent belief that if I could heal my own body/mind and spirit with nature, that I could truly make a difference in this world by assisting others who also believed in their body's innate wisdom to heal. I was only an infant of three months when my 25 year-old mother died at the hands of naive medical doctors who fed her drugs to treat the symptom of a misdiagnosed condition. My life forever changed at that moment of her death.

On some level, whether consciously or not, I saw it as my mission to prevent for others, the kind of suffering that my family endured as the result of unnecessary medical practices.

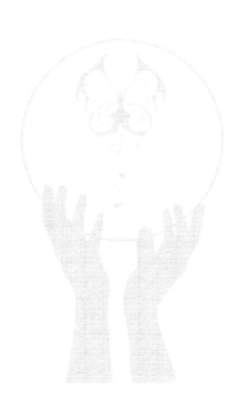

INTRODUCTION

When someone writes a piece of fiction, he or she is often asked whether it is autobiographical, if the characters are "real" people in the author's life, or how much of the story is based on the author's experiences. This book is not a piece of fiction, but I will tell you up front that it is real, it is autobiographical. It reflects who I am, what I have learned, what I teach and live each day, and, because I have written it down, what I hope others will embrace as part of their lives as well. I wish this because a part of my development as a physician/teacher has been the pursuit of knowledge and wisdom and the desire to share it with others. It became clear to me early in my career that there is a great need for people to know that they have the right to choose their own health care and that there is information available to help them make those choices. Through public speaking and my Center for Natural Healing, I have been sharing information regarding naturopathic and complementary medicine options for people of all ages. The Wisdom of Well-Being and Longevity Seminar Series is the fruit of my efforts to bring health care choices to the public. Top presenters on Mind-Body-Spirit related topics join me regularly to present nutritional recommendations, yogic breathing, and spiritual insights. In short, my goal is to teach Superhealth, how people can be in charge of their health and recognize their inborn capacity for greatness and inner peace, happiness, and well-being.

To facilitate that goal, many of the topics covered in this book are the same ones discussed in our seminars. Each entry is a snapshot of a way to reach Superhealth, of a way to visualize your end result by taking small, critical steps to master your nutrition, natural hygiene, leisure time, and thoughts, and to realize how unconditional love and unconditional forgiveness (of self and others) helps us to heal and enhance our personal and physical relationships.

We often have limiting beliefs about how good we can feel, how happy we can be, and how much energy we can have. Many of these barriers seem to be based on fear: fear of loss, fear of death, fear of being alone, fear of the unknown. These beliefs can in turn impact our physical well-being, manifesting as dis-ease like depression, chronic fatigue, heart disease, and asthma.

This book is about recognizing that there are no limits to what you can attain. It can be a tool to help you identify those fears, to acknowledge them and thank them for protecting you until now—and then just move through them, because they no longer serve you.

As you move through your fears, it can be easy to get caught up in the "doing" of living. That was my life for many years. In an effort to overcompensate for my perceived shortcomings and insecurities, I was constantly striving to do more and accomplish more. In the process I did not allow myself time to relax, reflect, or to cultivate relationships, including the one with myself. I forgot about my being-ness.

That is when I made the conscious decision to heal myself, my soul. I now focus my attention on how I am being as a friend, a mother, a doctor, an employer, a functional part of society. I am uncovering parts of myself that I have been hiding. I am certain there are more to be found. It is an adventure!

When we are busy doing, we are unaware of how our ego-driven plans can offend others and impact the subtle energies of those closest to us. From my new awareness of being-ness, I am learning to be more, better, and different as a human being. It is a lesson we can all learn.

Each of us harbors the seeds of every conceivable human characteristic in some ratio, however small they may be. Therefore, if we judge others we are admitting to the same quality within ourselves. These characteristics are our shadow sides: we all have these shadows, and they are visible to others. When we recognize this and allow ourselves to become honest and transparent, we are offering a gift to ourselves and to others. When we admit our faults, insecurities, and perceived imperfections, others will feel free to drop their guard and be more authentic with us.

You are a unique human being, blessed with something no human-designed computer can match—creativity. You have the power to think and create—there is no match for the human mind anywhere in the known universe. Yet some people strive to conform, to stay "WNL," within normal limits. When you reach out beyond those limits and tap into your creativity, your imagination, you can transcend your "average" or "normal" self and evolve into a person you may never have dreamed of becoming, until now.

Aristotle defined living things in terms of their potential, not what they were, but rather, what they could become.

What will you become? What is your divine purpose and potential? It is time to give yourself permission to grow, to achieve your highest potential. You were made perfect: celebrate your perfection. I invite you to join me on this quest for self, for greatness, for being-ness, for Superhealth.

BEGIN EACH DAY WITH QUIET PRAYERS & BLESSINGS

What are your first thoughts when you open up your eyes to greet the morning? Are you grateful for the opportunity to spend another joyful day contributing your best self to the world? Are you thankful for the restful hours of sleep that will enable you to spring out of bed with a vigorous zest for living, loving, and enjoying each waking moment?

Perhaps yes… or, perhaps you are not quite there yet. Either way, the thoughts, shares, lessons, and research provided in this and the following chapters, are designed to assist you in reclaiming your most vibrant, alert, energetic, enthusiastic, loving self, so that you may share YOU with the world. The YOU that you want to be.

4

Health and healing require paying attention to certain laws. Laws pertaining to the way our thoughts, words, and behaviors create what shows up in our daily lives. Whether involving our physical, emotional, spiritual, psychic or mental health, the way we think and the degree to which we take responsibility for our thoughts will have a direct impact on our health, at all levels.

Let's start our day, this day, by being fully aware of this most powerful and fundamental law of the universe. It is the law that states, "As we thinketh… so we shall become."

Pay attention to your thoughts. Whatever you are thinking about in any given moment is your contribution to the universe. Are you contributing in a way that you can be proud of, or are you part of a problem that may already be immense? You may shift at any moment. You may choose to focus on something pleasant. Notice the fresh air passing by your nostrils. Hear the sound of birds outside the window. See the sun, the clouds and the sky and think about the miracle and perfection of nature all around you. Starting your day slowly in quiet thought, gratitude and with love in your heart, not for any one in particular, just for your life, might be a gentler way of being than just springing out of bed.

If you drove your car up to full speed as soon as you turned it on, you would cause damage to the vehicle, reduce its ability to function properly and most likely cause an accident. Similarly, starting your day with a jolt will create disharmony, physically, spiritually, and emotionally and cause an uneasy, unbalanced foundation for the rest of your day.

Many people make the mistake of getting up and getting busy right away, or they lie in bed and mull over all the tasks they need to tackle that day. Both of these approaches can leave one feeling exhausted and stressed in a matter of minutes. Not only are these practices counterproductive in terms of work, they also place a strain on your overall health.

Instead, before you take on the business of the day's tasks, reflect on your "being". Think about how you want to "be" that day rather than what you need to do. How you want to "be" is a bigger and more important question than what you need to do. When you come from a place of Being, everything you do is a reflection of who you are, your "beingness." If you are unconscious of how you are being, your life will become a non-engaging series of tasks. You will become stressed, hurried, and disconnected from your surroundings.

The first thing I do when I wake is thank God for giving me another day, another chance to live life closer to my highest values and in greater integrity. Remember, we get more of what we appreciate and acknowledge. Reflect on the people in your life—children, partner, dear friends, yourself—the time you can spend with them, and how you want to show up for them. If you think about this ahead of time, you have a much better chance to make the most of the time you are together— and that includes the time you spend with yourself.

During these quiet moments, think about all the ways that you are blessed. It is all too easy to slip into a negative thought pattern: thinking about what you don't have, what makes you angry, what makes you sad. Our thoughts dictate our words; our words create our actions; our actions create our habits; our habits formulate our personality; our personality dictates our life and our life creates our destiny. It all starts with our thoughts. Living in gratitude might be easier accomplished if you consider some shocking statistics.

If you could shrink the entire world's population to a village of 100 people, retaining all existing human ratios, the village would look like this:

- 80 people living in substandard housing

- 70 people unable to read

- 50 suffering from malnutrition

- 4 without a home

- 1 with a college education

- 1 would own a computer

When we look at the world from this perspective, it becomes glaringly evident how blessed we are. Resolve to complain less. Hold up your head, smile, and be truly thankful for all of your good fortune. True happiness comes from embracing what you already have, not in getting what you think you want.

REFRESH YOURSELF WITH PURE WATER

When the well is dry, we know the worth of water.

–Benjamin Franklin, Poor Richard's Almanac 1746

When you look into a mirror, you see flesh, structure, and strength; yet the majority of your body is fluid, composed of 75 percent water, similar to the planet Earth. And your brain? It is 83 percent water. The mere fact that water makes up such a critical portion of your physical being is reason enough to ensure you provide the body with the most critical nutrient. Remember, like attracts like. Our cells need more of that which they are made of to stay alive. For that reason, it is also useful to examine the quality of the water being consumed.

Alas, many people do not. They turn on the tap and watch the chlorinated stream that typically also contains rust, sediment, fluoride, nitrate, arsenic, and even residuals of pharmaceutical medicines. In many places, there is an acceptable amount of human feces allowed in the "drinkable" water supply. Bottled water may or may not be much better. As consumers, we don't really know where the water came from, what has been added to it or filtered out, or how many chemicals from the plastic have leached into the water contained in our "purified" water bottles. The bottled water industry has rapidly become a multi-billion dollar industry. There are many claims about its purity and the health benefits contained within. As with all products on the market, as a buyer, we must beware.

When I ask my patients how much water they drink every day, they typically admit "not enough." Often they will say they don't think about drinking water because they are not thirsty. This indicates that the individual has gone so long without drinking enough water that their receptors for thirst are not functioning at full capacity. This is particularly evident in the elderly population. Many elderly individuals only drink enough to get their pills down. They don't want to be inconvenienced by the need to use the bathroom, especially because so many elderly are placed on diuretics to drain the inflammation in their bodies caused by lack of water. This creates a severe dehydration that no pill can fix. Often times, by skipping the pills and drinking water, can create more health for the person than they can remember experiencing since the inception of their diagnosis.

Being aware that you need to drink more water is half the battle; the other half is taking action. Your body needs water to perform a countless number of critical processes. If it does not get enough—at least 64 ounces per day—your brain will draw on water reserves in the body, leaving you dehydrated and at risk for conditions such as gastritis, heartburn, ulcers, and ulcerative colitis. These inflammatory conditions develop because of an imbalance in the system that cannot be cured by pharmaceutical medicine. The simplest solution would be to restore the proper nutrient and fluid balance in the body. This will in turn heal the delicate mucus membrane linings of the body, thus preventing or resolving inflammation.

Consuming water that will assist the body in neutralizing the acid waste that is accumulated in the system, is an effective way of satisfying two important goals simultaneously.

One revolutionary way to achieve this goal is by drinking ionized, alkaline water. Water that is extracted from an ionizer hydrates our cells more effectively, due to the micro-clustering of water molecules. These micro-clustered molecules are the negatively charged water molecules that bind to the free-radically damaged positively charged particles floating around in the system which enable their effective elimination.

Every morning, greet the day by drinking pure, ionized water at room temperature. Iced water destroys the enzymes in the body that are needed for digestion, absorption, assimilation, elimination, and utilization of nutrients. Ionized water helps to balance the body's pH of which the most desirable level is 7.4. All sodas and sports drinks, including Gatorade, PowerAde and even "Smart Water" have a pH in the acidic range. The more sugar, flavor and artificial ingredients, chemicals and preservatives, the greater the acidity of the product. In an acidic body, healthy cells do not thrive.

In 1931, Dr. Otto Warburg won a Nobel Prize for discovering the real cause of cancer. Dr. Warburg was the director of the Kaiser Wilhelm Institute, now the Max Planck Institute for cell physiology in Berlin. He investigated the metabolism of tumors and the respiration of cells, particularly cancer cells.

"Cancerous tissues are acidic, whereas healthy tissues are alkaline." In his work "The Metabolism of Tumors", Warburg demonstrated that all forms of cancer are characterized by two basic conditions: acidosis and hypoxia (lack of oxygen); and where you have one, you have the other. He stated that "all normal cells have an absolute requirement for oxygen, except cancer cells which live without oxygen—a rule without exception."

This gives us another imperative reason to exercise and be conscious of our breathing. Deep inhalations through our nose provide the most optimal cellular oxidation. Mouth breathing tends to be shallow and the result of chronic sinus congestion which must not be overlooked as a naturopathically treatable condition. Do you sometimes feel restless, stiff, overwhelmed, unfocused, confused, weak, and/or overtired? These are indications that the body's pH may be too acidic and out of its normal healthy balance. A body that is too acidic provides an ideal environment for diseases to take hold and thrive. Drinking pure ionized water helps restore balance, as does walking in nature while breathing deeply into your cells. These two simple, yet imperative practices, assist in the prevention of disease. There are many available models of water alkalinizers on the market. For more information on ordering a machine that will provide quality, clean, medicinal hydration for you and your family for as little as three to six cents per day, please contact me.

START EACH DAY WITH FRESH WHEATGRASS

Wheatgrass is a live food, and when you begin each day with a few ounces of fresh wheatgrass, you share in the energy of the sun and earth. Many people find that wheatgrass juice gives them a spiritual, physical, and emotional boost that lasts throughout the day.

Although three ounces of wheatgrass contains a fair amount of vitamin A, calcium, magnesium, and other nutrients, the main source of its healing benefits come from chlorophyll. Ann Wigmore, the great humanitarian and founder of the Hippocrates Health Institute, was an avid advocate of wheatgrass and wrote extensively on its virtues. First and foremost, wheatgrass juice is 70 percent chlorophyll, an element that contains more light energy than any other. Like all green plants that contain chlorophyll, wheatgrass is high in oxygen. It is an easily digestible food, as it uses very little energy to assimilate with your body. This makes it a perfect food with which to start your day.

The chlorophyll in wheatgrass can provide many gifts of health. It contains antibacterial properties that are effective both inside the body and when used topically. Thus wheatgrass juice can help eliminate bacteria throughout your digestive system and gastrointestinal tract as well as on your skin and mucous membranes. Chlorophyll can enter body tissues; rebuild low red blood cell levels due to its molecular structure which mimics the "heme" molecule of hemoglobin in the blood. Wheatgrass in its fresh form assists the body in neutralizing toxins, aids the pancreas in glucose regulation and rejuvenates cells.

Wheatgrass is useful as part of a detoxification program for anyone wishing to achieve greater clarity, energy or vitality. As with any substance used for cleansing and detoxifying, it is necessary to be alert to possible signs of cleansing that may appear to be adverse. These symptoms may be part of a "healing crisis" that occurs when many toxins are dumped into the bloodstream at once. Some of the symptoms may be expressed as headaches, irritability, traveling pains, vomiting, diarrhea, fatigue, fever or chills.

Consulting with a qualified, licensed doctor specializing in cleansing and detoxification prior to initiating a detox program is recommended. Be sure to check the credentials of anyone advertising themselves as a holistic practitioner and confirm that they are licensed and trained properly through an accredited Naturopathic Medical Institute.

Often times when we attempt to put ourselves on a cleansing program, we are unsuccessful because we are not equipped with the knowledge of the necessary preliminary steps that prepare our immune systems for such a cleanse. Our immune system must be strong enough to handle the extra burden, otherwise we may become sick.

Think of all the animals that eat grass and how strong and healthy they are. Now think about the house cat that will eat grass when not feeling well. Inherently he knows that if he eats the grass, he will throw up. This is his goal. It is his healing. He does not go into crisis. He will then go and rest. The cat knows how much grass to eat to produce the desired result. When we as humans become as instinctually in-tune with our bodies and less easily swayed by propaganda and the influence of our social conditioning, we will also know how to eat, drink and treat ourselves to ensure perfect health and balance. As far back as 1940, chlorophyll was recommended in the American Journal of Surgery to neutralize streptococcal infections, heal wounds, treat chronic inner ear inflammation and infections, cure chronic sinusitis, eliminate parasitic and vaginal infections, and clear up foul-smelling odors. Wheatgrass is still considered by many to be one of Nature's most healing foods. It helps my patients who have digestive problems, especially ulcers, liver diseases, and cancers. Wheatgrass also helps individuals increase their stamina and mental alertness. Wheatgrass juice is great on its own. Due to its high concetration of chlorophyll, it is far superior to carrot juice, maple syrup and cayenne pepper, or the juice of other fruits and vegetables when it comes to detoxification. It is best to drink wheatgrass juice first thing in the morning or on an empty stomach. Growing your own wheatgrass is a wonderful way to connect with your food, and it is easy to do. There are wheatgrass growing kits on the market, but you can also get instructions online or in books on wheatgrass, including Ann Wigmore's classic, The Wheatgrass Book: How to Grow and Use Wheatgrass to Maximize Your Health and Vitality or you may call The Center for Natural Healing for literature on the subject. Research scientist Dr. Max Bircher, founder of the Bircher-Benner Clinic in Zurich, calls chlorophyll "concentrated sun power." He says that "Chlorophyll increases the function of the heart, affects the vascular system, the intestines, the uterus, and the lungs. It is therefore a tonic which, considering its stimulating properties, cannot be compared with any other."

For all these reasons and more, I encourage you to include wheatgrass juice as part of your daily routine. Your body will thank you for it!

EXERCISE DAILY

I know you have heard this advice many times, but do you really know why exercise is so important? The human body was made to move. Its many thousands of muscles, bones, tendons, ligaments, and approximately 100,000 miles of blood vessels are enveloped by an instrument that's meant to be played every day.

There are multiple benefits of regular exercise for physical health. Here are just a few. Physical activity reduces stress, lowers blood pressure, improves flexibility, enhances blood circulation, strengthens the heart, tones the muscles, relieves pain by pumping endorphins into your system, helps with weight loss, strengthens bones, improves quality of sleep, relieves menstrual cramps, and much, much more.

On a mental and emotional level, exercise improves concentration, sharpens awareness, stimulates creativity, enriches sexuality, boosts self-esteem, relieves depression, and helps with decision-making. Spiritually, it can make you feel more in touch with your higher power, your environment, and your beingness.

These are amazing fringe benefits to the exhilaration you can derive from fitness routine that you enjoy, however let's talk about why physical activity is so imperative. Within our body is contained a lymphatic system, which is a network of capillaries that parallels the blood vessels. Unlike the cardiovascular system through which blood is pumped and moved through the vessels by the heart, the lymph system has no pump. The lymph system is designed to filter out the toxins from the body, like the lint filter of your dryer. Unfortunately, without exercise, once stored, these toxins remain trapped inside the lymph vessels.

When they have overstayed their welcome to the point where the body becomes worn down from too much toxic accumulation, combined with lack of sleep, stress, low energy, a passing virus, or bacterial invasion, the body will do one of two things: encapsulate the toxins in the lymph channels to create swollen lymph nodes, and/or cause a break down in the system which will manifest in illness or disease.

This is exactly what we want to prevent.

Many people say the challenge for them is "finding the time" or "making the time" to exercise. In reality, it is not about finding or making anything. It's about managing your time wisely so you can incorporate physical exercise into your lifestyle. Exercise should also be a relaxing, enjoyable activity, not one that you dread or suffer anxiety about doing—these feelings are counterproductive.

Therefore, it is important to choose activities that bring you joy, find others you can share that enjoyment with, and allow yourself options so you do not get bored or frustrated. If you find it difficult to set aside a 30 or 45 minute period of time each day to exercise, you might divide your activities into two sessions: perhaps a brisk walk in the morning or during lunch and aerobics before dinner. Swimming, if you have access to a pool or, better yet, in the ocean, is an excellent form of exercise. Perhaps you derive joy from walking or tennis, dance, jogging, or skiing. If you have fun with a treadmill or stepping machine, go for it! Remember it is easier to create a habit if it is enjoyable. It takes 21 days to make your new health habit stick. Creating new healthy habits to replace old sedentary habits is critical.

Physical exercise is a holistic experience. If you look at it with that in mind, you will reap more than physical rewards; you will engage your emotional, mental, and spiritual self as well.

YOUR SKIN IS A REFLECTION OF YOUR INTERNAL SYSTEM

The skin is the largest organ of the body, and it is constantly touched by all elements it is exposed to. Thus every soap, lotion, article of clothing, air pollutant, or type of water that makes contact with your skin can have an impact on its appearance and health. Your skin may respond by absorbing the substance, being irritated by it, or by being affected in some other way. Your task is to ensure that your skin is healthy and vital so it can optimally perform its important functions.

Those functions are essential for your overall health and include serving as a major protector against invading micro-organisms and toxins. At the same time, your skin is the largest organ of elimination, and so it is also responsible for getting rid of toxins and other unwelcome substances through the pores when you sweat. When the skin is functioning at its best, it gets rid of about two pounds of acid waste daily.

To ensure your skin can perform its very best and look great involves keeping it clean using natural cleansing methods. I suggest you start by using a natural fiber cloth or a soft, natural bristle brush to exfoliate your skin before you shower. This eliminates dead skin cells and allows for and enhances detoxification. Use of a dry brush or cloth also improves blood circulation and circulation of lymph, the clear, watery fluid, that plays an important role in protecting the body against viruses, bacteria, and other invading micro-organisms. A good brushing also reduces puffiness and calms the nervous system. After you brush your body with a dry brush or cloth, you can add a natural soap to wash yourself. Use a circular motion and begin with your face, ears, and neck, and move down your body. Spend a little extra time on your legs and feet, which can improve circulation and elimination of toxins. A lingering, circular motion can also help reduce cellulite, which is the accumulation of waste products under skin, mixed with intracellular fluids.

Now about your soap: look for soaps that contain natural, organic ingredients, such as essential oil, cold-pressed olive oil, organic herbs, beeswax, green tea, jojoba oil, oats, sea salt, vitamin E, and yucca root, among others. Avoid products that contain synthetics (including artificial fragrances), petroleum products, dyes, and preservatives. Remember, your skin will absorb these toxins.

Treating your body with respect includes using natural soaps, scrubbing cloths and brushes that are kind to your skin. Along with a nutritious diet, exercise and stress management practices, taking care of your skin will leave you with a radiant glow of health and vitality.

SCRUB YOUR NAILS

Did your mother always tell you to scrub under your nails? The area under your fingernails and toenails are havens for bacteria and other microorganisms and debris that can transmit disease. We are reminded repeatedly to wash our hands, but if you don't scrub under your nails, you have not finished the job.

How often we touch our eyes and faces, without being aware of what is breeding under our nails. There are two tools you can use. One is a nail file to clean under your nails. The other tool is a nail brush, which you can use to clean your fingernails with soap during the day or before bed. You can do the same for your toenails, although you may choose to care for them in the shower or tub. To remove dead skin and other debris from the bottom of your feet, I suggest using a pumice stone.

Always clean your brushes and nail tools, just like you rinse out your toothbrush. Occasionally you may wish to put all your brushes in the dishwasher. You can also soak brushes overnight in water with a pH of 2.5 to 4.0, which can be obtained from many water ionizers. This level of pH is excellent for sanitizing your brushes and nail file (as well as your sponges, dish cloths, cutting boards, and other items that may need sanitizing).

BREATHE!

When the Breath wanders, the mind is unsteady, but when the Breath is still, so is the mind still.

–Hatha Yoga Pradipika

Without breath there is no life, yet we take breathing for granted until something happens that hinders our ability to breathe properly. Thus it is a good idea to take time each day to celebrate the very act of breathing, to learn how to breathe properly and to honor the life-giving, life-sustaining essence of each inhalation and exhalation.

Because breathing is so essential for life, it is in the best interest of your physical, spiritual, emotional, and mental health to do it the very best way you can so you can derive the most benefit from it. Pranayama, or breathing exercise, is one of the five principles of yoga, and it promotes proper breathing.

According to the Yogic perspective, proper breathing brings more oxygen to the blood and to the brain, and it also controls the vital life energy, or Prana. When we breathe in, we take in oxygen which then passes through the body in a form that revitalizes everything it touches. Then we exhale carbon dioxide and release toxins from the body. The practice of Pranayama helps you absorb vital life energy through breath control, linking your body, mind, and spirit.

When we are under stress, our breathing tends to be fast and shallow, and we do not get all the oxygen the body needs. A lack of sufficient oxygen can contribute to many health problems, including heart disease, sleep disorders, lack of concentration, and fatigue, to name a few. When we breathe properly, we revitalize the body, mind, and spirit.

Here is an explanation of the yoga complete breath.

• Sit on the edge of a chair with your feet flat. Throughout the exercise, always breathe through your nose and concentrate on the sound of your breath.

• Place your hands on your abdomen and breathe out; do not slouch forward. Tighten your belly muscles to release as much air as possible.

• Begin to breathe in from the bottom up; allowing your belly muscles to relax so the air seems to fill your belly.

• Continue to breathe in until you feel the air has filled you up to the top of your lungs

• Now gently and slowly begin to breathe out, beginning at the top. First relax your chest, then your ribs, and finally tighten your belly and push out the last bit of air.

• The entire cycle—from the initial breathing in to the final pushing out of breath—may take 10 to 30 seconds. Strive to breathe in and out for about the same length of time.

• Practice yoga complete breath 5 to 10 repetitions once a day (takes 2-4 minutes) and gradually work up to five or ten minutes of practice daily.

Breathing is the only way we have to deliver life-sustaining oxygen to the body. Yoga complete breathing can help you get the most benefit from every breath you take.

BREAK YOUR FAST WITH FRESH FRUIT

There is greater relish for the earliest fruit of the season.

–Marcus Valerius Martialis, Roman poet (38-103 AD)

After a night of sleep, the best and most delightful way to get your digestive juices flowing is to introduce one of nature's perfect foods: fruit. Fresh fruit is likely the very first food that humans consumed, long before legumes, grains, meat, and dairy. All they had to do was reach out and pick from a tree, bush, or vine, and the sweetness of sunlight and juicy pulp was ready for them to enjoy.

Fresh fruits are the best foods to start your day because they are easy to digest, so they do not shock the body out of its slumber mode and the quietude from your morning meditation. Why? Because fruit is composed of simple sugars, many vitamins and minerals and lots of water which assimilate into the body very quickly. This allows the body to remain in its detoxification mode longer, rather than demanding heavy digestive processes first thing in the morning. According to the laws of proper food combining, eating fresh fruit on an empty stomach is most beneficial for digestion. It is further recommended, especially if you have sensitive digestive systems, to eat one type of fruit at a time, as different families of fruit require different enzymes for digestion.

This just assists the body in slowly waking up rather than necessitating a great deal of energy. People who eat fruit along with or after a meal often experience digestive problems because the fruit sugar is "trapped" in the stomach with the other food components and it begins to ferment. This may cause bloating or gas formation.

Fruit is a simple, whole food that is best to be consumed in an equally simple manner: one kind at a time.

• Citrus fruits combine well together, oranges, grapefruit, lemons, and tangerines, and are best eaten separate from other categories of fruit.

• Melons should always be eaten alone as well

• Strawberries and kiwi are in the same family and can be eaten together. Other beneficial combinations are:

• Blueberries, raspberries, and blackberries

• Sweet apples, sweet peaches, sweet cherries

• Pears, papayas, mangoes

• Apricots, sweet plums, fresh figs (but not dried)

• Bananas and sweet grapes

When you begin your day with fresh fruit, you gently awaken

your body's digestive system to its task and ease into your day with sweetness, nutrition, and lightness.

CHEW, CHEW, CHEW!

Chewing the food of sweet and bitter fancy.

–William Shakespeare, As You Like It

Here is an activity we don't think about enough, chewing. The act of chewing is the first step in the digestive process, so it pays to do the very best you can so the rest of the journey will be as smooth and efficient as possible.

A presiding principle is to chew all foods close to a liquid consistency before you swallow. This is the best way known to help digestion at this stage of the process. Yet most people do not chew their food properly, and many combine this habit with eating much too quickly as well. Both of these practices contribute to indigestion and poor absorption of nutrients.

Did you know that if you swallow a grape or cherry whole, it will usually pass through the entire system whole? This would negate any nutrients from being absorbed.

There are other benefits to chewing your food thoroughly. When you eat slowly, you pay attention to your food; in fact, chewing slowly and thoughtfully can be a form of mindfulness meditation. When you are mindful of your food you can enjoy it more thoroughly. Consider a fresh salad bowl, filled with red leaf lettuce, onions, bell peppers, cherry tomatoes, crisp cucumber slices, black olives, grated carrot, broccoli florets, and alfalfa sprouts, sprinkled with sunflower kernels and a tangy vinaigrette dressing. If you eat it quickly and don't take the time to chew, chew, chew, you will miss out on the wonderful dichotomy of textures and flavors. You will not realize how the lettuce complements the onion, the tomatoes pop in your mouth, and the cucumber slices snap. How does the dressing enhance the flavor of each and every vegetable? You will never know if you rush through your meal.

Here is another benefit associated with chewing your food well; it can help you maintain your ideal body weight. A growing number of studies confirm that when you eat slowly, you tend to consume fewer calories. That's because it takes about 20 minutes for the brain to realize that you are full. If you eat quickly, you are much more likely to continue eating past the point where you are full. Food is your body's fuel. Deliver it in a form it can utilize most efficiently. Chew your food well, and it will serve you well.

SCRAPE YOUR TONGUE

I want you to have clean tongues, clean manners, clean morals and clean characters. –John Burns

Have you ever tried scraping your tongue? If not, I am willing to guess you will be very pleasantly surprised to discover just how refreshed your mouth will feel. And once you learn about the importance of cleaning your tongue, you will probably feel even better!

You may already know that in Chinese medicine, the tongue is a very important organ to practitioners. Beyond being the site of taste receptor cells that allow us to taste, the tongue also serves other functions. Its appearance can change with physiological changes in the body, and so the appearance of the tongue is like a canvas that reveals how the body is functioning. A knowledgeable practitioner can "read" your tongue and detect imbalances in different systems in the body.

The tongue is also a collection site for bacteria and other minute substances. In fact, the majority of the bacteria that cause bad breath live on the tongue, among the miniscule little bumps called papillae and the grooves between them. While the papillae are topped with taste buds, bacteria settle into the grooves and set up residence. If you scrape your tongue, you uproot those unwelcome "guests" and prevent them from causing bad breath. Removing them is also best for your overall health and can improve your sense of taste as well.

But, you say, I already use an antibacterial mouthwash. Doesn't that kick out the bacteria? Yes, use of a quality natural mouthwash is a fine idea, but scraping your tongue is still recommended. Here's why. Some bacteria are anaerobes, which means they live and thrive in environments deprived of oxygen, like the grooves between the papillae. These bacteria break down protein, which produces a terrible odor, hence bad breath.

Protein in the mouth comes from many sources: from molecules of saliva, dead skin cells from the inside of your mouth, food particles, and inflammatory cells that lurk in the mouth. These protein-chomping, odor-producing bacteria are actually protected by a thin layer of material that coats the tongue and prevents these bacteria from being removed, that is, unless you scrape your tongue. It is also a good idea to follow each tongue scraping with an oral rinse.

To scrape your tongue, all you need is a teaspoon, or you can buy a tongue scraper, available in most pharmacies and online. To use a teaspoon, hold it upside down so that the rounded edge touches your tongue. You will love how refreshed your mouth will feel and your loved ones will most definitely notice a change in your "aroma". Best of all, you will get to watch the bacteria that used to live in your mouth get rinsed down the drain.

LAUGH YOUR WAY TO BETTER HEALTH

You have heard the cliché—laughter is the best medicine—and it is, so true. There is nothing like a good belly laugh to lift your spirits, lower your blood pressure, relieve discomfort, improve job performance, and make your blood vessels work better. Honestly, that's what the research says. Bet you didn't know a good laugh can do all that. Laughter is also a wonderful salve for wounded relationships and communication, as it synchronizes the brains of the people involved so they are emotionally in tune. In fact, some researchers believe one of the main purposes of laughter is to bring people together.

One of the most impressive and interesting benefits of laughter, along with a good sense of humor, is its ability to protect the heart and blood vessels. Research indicates that laughter has an impact on the inner lining of the blood vessels, called the endothelium, and allows them to relax and expand. This increases blood flow throughout the body, including the brain. The endothelium also adjusts the ability of the blood to clot, and it secretes various chemicals when an injury or infection occurs. Therefore scientists proposed that laughing may help maintain a healthy endothelium and, by extension, reduce the risk of cardiovascular disease.

Even if none of this were true—though indications are strong— laughter is a wonderful stress buster and is just plain fun. When you are laughing it is difficult to be angry, too, and anger and hostility are associated with an increased risk of heart disease.

A study conducted at St. Cloud State University in Minnesota in 2009 reported that there are three main theories to explain the functions of humor: relief, incongruity, and superiority. Although these theories focus on the specific role humor plays for people in various situations, the study's authors noted that the bottom line was that there are physiological benefits of laughter, and that these benefits occur regardless of which theory applies. Laughter heals. Laughter brings joy. It brings people together and perhaps helps them live longer. Laughter is free—free to share, to explore, to enjoy, to cultivate. Laugh long, often, and loud.

CLEAR YOUR SINUSES

You may be thinking, "I don't have any trouble with my sinuses,so why do I need to worry about clearing them?" I'm glad you asked. One reason is the increasing pollution and chemicals in the environment that are contributing to a growing number of people who are experiencing allergies, nasal congestion, and respiratory problems. Do you often have a stuffy nose, headache, or pressure in your sinuses? These are symptoms that clearing your sinuses daily can help prevent. If you do experience occasional or frequent sinus infections, then this is an ideal way to help prevent and manage them. A sinus infection is caused by bacteria within the sinus cavities. The infection can cause a mild to severe headache in the sinus area behind the eyes, forehead, and check bones, along with a stuffy nose. Yes, you can take one of many different sinus infection medications or herbs that are available over the counter, but by clearing your sinuses regularly, even daily, you may never need to take them again, or only infrequently. Remember, all pharmaceutical medicine predisposes one to a variety of side effects. Many people use a neti pot to rinse their sinuses. A neti pot is a vessel that resembles a small tea pot. The practice of neti to rinse the sinuses originated in India, but it is widely used today around the world. As part of a comprehensive health program, I often recommend the regular practice of nasal cleansing because it is a good way to eliminate pollutants, pollen, dust, mucous, and other irritants from your nose and sinuses. Here is the "recipe" for sinus cleansing: ½ teaspoon sea salt, 8 ounces pure, ionized water at room temperature or ½ teaspoon baking soda. Mix the ingredients in a clean container. Pour some of the mixture it into your neti pot or the palm of your hand. If you use a neti pot, tilt your head sideways and place the spout into one nostril. Tilt the pot so the water comes out the other nostril. You may see some mucous in the water when it comes out. Keep rinsing your sinuses until you no longer see any mucous. Repeat for the other nostril. If you prefer not to use a neti pot, you can use your hand. Just put a little salt water in your palm and sniff it up into your nostrils, then move your head around to allow the water to circulate in your nasal passages. Not just any salt will do! I find that the best salt for clearing the sinuses is sea salt. Gargling with salt water is also an effective remedy for a sore or swollen throat and for decreasing inflammation. The salt water in the ocean is one of the most antimicrobial substances in the world. The ocean mist is full of negative ions that are beneficial to breathe into your body. You can enjoy many of the same benefits when you use sea salt.

Newcomers to sinus cleansing sometimes experience some coughing after rinsing their sinuses because some of the fluid may drain down the back of their throat. With practice this discomfort will diminish.

HEED THE CALL OF NATURE

You know it happens; you are in the middle of something important, like a board meeting, so you put off going to the bathroom. Or you are driving and you decide you can wait rather than stop somewhere. Or you are with a group of people and you don't want to make everyone wait for you while you go to the bathroom.

Delaying or stopping yourself from moving your bowels or urinating when Nature calls is a very unhealthy habit. For the most part, your body is pretty sophisticated; it knows when your bowels and bladder are full and need to be emptied. If all systems are operating relatively smoothly, you get sufficient warning about the need to eliminate. Your body sends signals that get more and more intense as time passes in the case of urination. However, the colon really only sends one major signal that it is time to go.

If you make a habit of ignoring these signals, your brain will automatically ease up on sending this crucial information. The end result could be constipation. Over time, pockets may form collecting the stool that was not eliminated in a timely fashion, hence the diagnosis of diverticulitis. This is a toxic condition. When waste is harbored in the intestinal tract, several unpleasant things happen. The spoiling waste promotes unfriendly microorganisms and parasites whose by-products can enter the blood stream. You can begin to feel moody, gassy, and bloated. The longer the wastes stay in your body, the more your entire system is compromised, and your energy level can drop dramatically. If you hold urine for a long time and often, you can get a urinary tract infection or a distended bladder, which means it cannot contract as well as it should and it will not empty properly. If this should happen to you, you can help get your bladder back into shape by following a schedule of frequent urination. Go to the bathroom every two to three hours during the day to keep your bladder empty most of the time. This will allow it to regain its integrity.

So when Nature calls, answer as quickly as possible. There are several things you can do to help this process.

• Before leaving the house or office, go to the bathroom, even if you don't feel like you have to go.

• If you are on a road trip, use the facilities every time you stop, even if you don't need to go.

• Pay attention to the timing of your liquid intake, especially caffeine, if you will not be near a bathroom. Caffeinated beverages like coffee and tea can increase your need to urinate. Do not, however, dehydrate yourself.

- When you go to a large public facility or outdoor venue, such as a shopping mall or park, learn where the bathroom facilities are so you will be prepared when Nature calls.

Drinking ample water is crucial for both bowel and kidney function to perform regularly.

CHECK YOUR POSTURE

Stand up straight! How many times did you hear that when you were growing up? As a child you probably rolled your eyes whenever you heard that admonishment, but with age you likely came to realize that it was good advice. Your posture is the physical result of how you balance your body. Your posture is unique to you—whether it is good or bad—and chances are it could be better or stronger than it is right now. Weak posture can be strengthened with exercise and a conscious effort to stay aware of your body and it's placement during exercise and when at rest. One thing that has a significant impact on posture is pain. Pain not only makes you move differently, it can actually change your posture because it causes you to compensate and place stress on other parts of your body. If you place undue stress on any part of your body for a prolonged period of time, it can cause it to wear down more quickly than nature intended. Conversely, if your posture is poor, it can cause pain, even arthritis and headache. Being overweight can also have a negative impact on posture.

Improving your posture means you need to teach your body to move in new, healthier ways. I don't expect you to think about your posture all day—no one can do that—but the secret is to program yourself to create new habits that improve your posture.

One way is to practice several posture-improving exercises each day. (You should check with your naturopathic doctor before participating in any exercise program.) These can include exercises that strengthen your core—your abdominal and back muscles—and exercises that help you hold your neck and shoulders in a better position.

Here is an exercise to get you started:

•   Stand against a wall with your feet shoulder width apart.

•   Gently press your lower back against the wall

•   Place the back of your elbows, forearms, and wrists against the wall

•   Raise your arms up and down slowly while keeping your elbows in contact with the wall

•   Repeat 8 to 10 times

Throughout the day, check in with yourself. How is my posture? Am I standing up straight? Good posture means your ears, shoulders, hips, and ankles all align in one straight line when you look at yourself in a mirror from the side. Avoid slouching and wearing heels that can result in unbalanced posture. If you experience any pain or discomfort while doing posture exercises, you should stop and consult your doctor. Posture exercises should be performed pain free. A physical therapist or other health professional can help you choose exercises that can improve your posture. And of course if none of these appeal to you, you may always join me at my next ballet class.

CHOOSE NATURAL, ORGANIC FOOD

Do you believe your body deserves the very best fuel possible? Then natural, organic foods are your best choice. Eating organic fruits, vegetables, and whole grains is important for several reasons. One is obvious, organic foods have far less pesticides than those grown and processed conventionally. Notice I did not say organic foods are pesticide-free. Foods that are grown organically may still be exposed unintentionally to runoff or wind-carried contaminants. Research shows, however, that conventionally grown fruits and vegetables are contaminated with a wide range of pesticides.

For example, in 2008 the Environmental Working Group tested 43 fruits and vegetables for pesticide residue. They found that nearly 100% of peaches examined had detectable pesticides, 86.6% had at least 2 pesticides, and 42 different pesticides were found among the entire sample. Other fruits and veggies did not fare much better, including apples, sweet peppers, celery, nectarines, cherries, lettuce, grapes, and pears rounding out the top ten.

Some studies show that organic foods are more nutritious than conventionally grown foods. Even though organic foods often cost a bit more, you get better value for your dollar, better nutrition without the toxins. It also is not necessary to eat as much when the quality is better. Less, as they say, is more. And taste, although subjective, many people who eat organic fruits and veggies say they taste better than conventionally grown produce. I am one of them.

While eating organic foods is good for everyone's health, they are especially important for the most vulnerable—children and pregnant and breast-feeding women. Children are more susceptible to the health impact of pesticides because their bodies are smaller and they often enjoy several foods that are among the most highly contaminated, including finger foods like grapes, strawberries, cherries, and apple and peach slices.

A study from the University of Washington in Seattle found that preschoolers who ate a conventional diet had six times the level of certain pesticides in their urine than children who ate organic foods. And there's more, a study from the Centers for Disease Control and Prevention found twice the level of some pesticides in the urine of children as in that of adults. Research also shows that pesticides can cross the placenta during pregnancy, where they can affect the developing organs and brain of the fetus. Infants and young children are also less able to eliminate contaminants from their bodies because their immune systems and livers are not yet fully developed.

What does "organic" mean? A label that says "100% organic" means the product is completely organic or made of all organic ingredients. "Organic" means the product is at least 95% organic. "Made with organic ingredients" means the product must contain at least 70% organic ingredients.

We owe it to ourselves and to the young people whose lives we influence, to eat foods that are as free of contaminants as possible. That includes avoiding processed, refined foods—those that contain preservatives, artificial flavorings and colorings, and ingredients that only a chemist could decipher.

GIVE THANKS EVERY DAY

When you woke up this morning, what was your first thought? Did you immediately think about all the work you had to do? Or which bills you had to pay? Or about the traffic you had to dodge to get to work? Or did you thank God, your higher power, or the Universe for your life?

When things in our life are going well, when life is easy, it is much easier to be thankful than when situations are not going our way. When the bills are piling up, traffic is backed up, the boss is on our back, and we feel like we're up against a wall, it can be hard to feel thankful.

We could begin by being thankful we are not living in the streets or starving to death. We could be thankful that we have all (or most) of our faculties, that our health is good (or not so bad). We could be thankful that the sun is warm on our face, and that we are alive.

It is a matter of perspective. When people experience terrible tragedies, such as a devastating earthquake or hurricane that destroys their home and all their belongings, it is not uncommon to hear survivors say, "We lost our house but we still have each other," or "It was just stuff. I still have my family."

We are blessed with a mind that allows us to be reflective, contemplative, and a heart that knows how to be grateful. If in the face of hardship, bad luck, heartbreak, and even devastation we are able to keep a healthy sense of perspective, we will be better able to appreciate what we do have, that it is precious, and then we can continue on with an attitude of thankfulness and gratitude.

When you find it difficult to find something for which to be thankful, here's a suggestion—take a walk. Walk somewhere you can be alone with yourself and nature. As you walk, make a list in your head of all the things for which you are thankful. They can be seemingly silly things: oatmeal cookies, your cat, and the trees. As you get "warmed up," you will likely think of other things: your best friend, your partner, your home, music, a favorite book, and the clouds. This simple yet powerful walk of gratitude can lift you out of the blues and self-pity.

If you don't have a place to walk, take the walk in your mind. Close your eyes and practice guided imagery. In your mind's eye, picture yourself in a beautiful, peaceful place and start walking and naming things for which you are grateful. This "walk" can be just as powerful as the physical act of putting one foot in front of the other.

If you have negative thought, say "cancel." Your subconscious takes commands. Replace the thoughts with gratitude. Remember the positive things that happen each day, and then plan to share them with someone.

There is abundance everywhere around us. Believe it, give thanks every day and abundance will always be with you.

SPEND TIME WITH NATURE

Get outside every day. Miracles are waiting everywhere.

One of the greatest of life's pleasures is the enjoyment of nature. Even if it is only for a 15 to 20 minute walk in a park or along a river, or perhaps in your own garden, we all need time away from the hustle and bustle of the daily demands from work, family, and the environment: noise, pollutants, crowds, phones, television, traffic, concrete, and steel. When we go out into nature, we can commune with the elements, connect with the primal force, and listen to the sounds of life.

Did you know that spending time in Nature makes people

more caring? That's what some researchers at the University of Rochester say, but if you have spent any time engaged with the natural environment, you may have already experienced such feelings of enlightenment, gratitude, and caring.

Taking the time to experience your natural surroundings has both social and personal benefits. Along with the increased feelings of caring, being in Nature also has a calming effect—it reduces stress and contributes to increased happiness and physical health.

Results of a recent study found that interacting with Nature requires a less demanding form of attention. When you switch over from the demands and stress of everyday life and enter a "nature mode," you can recharge your batteries. It is like taking a mini vacation.

I realize that everyone does not have the opportunity to submerge themselves in a natural setting each and every day. For people who live in a highly urbanized area, with little or no access to a park, the ocean, a lake, or gardens, the most chance they have of experiencing nature is on television or video. Although it is not ideal, watching a nature program on television or a video/DVD can be a substitute until you can experience the real thing.

And when you do get out into the "real thing," fully engage the experience. Focus on the sound of the breeze, the birds, and the water. Inhale the aromas of the earth and its creatures and flora. Taste the air or, if possible, the fruits of the earth.

Relish the sights and the colors, the horizon, and the sky. Touch the earth with your feet, the textures of rocks and trees, the coolness of a running brook, the sand between your fingers. Close your eyes and imagine you are one with Nature... because you are!

SOCIALIZE

Ah, we are complex creatures! Sometimes we want to be alone, isolate ourselves, shut ourselves away from family, friends, co-workers, and the world. Other times we seek company, someone with whom we can talk, share, complain, dream, and love. That is the social us, the "no man is an island" us. Social interaction is a key part of living well. Good friendships, family bonding, love relationships, and overall health all go hand-in-hand. I believe it is critical to have at least one friend with whom you can have heart-to-heart communication. If you do not, I also realize that such an individual is not someone you just "pick up" overnight; such relationships take a while to nurture and develop. But the process of establishing a close relationship with someone is immensely rewarding. Whether that individual is of the same gender or not, younger or older, does not matter if you "click" on issues, philosophies, and perspectives that are of importance to both of you. In fact, differences are good. They help us grow individually and socially; they can expand our minds and knowledge and help us be more tolerant and patient.

Too much solitude causes people to be preoccupied with themselves and to become too self-absorbed. Socializing is necessary to balance your emotional and spiritual health. We all know that staying physically fit is essential for good health, but staying socially fit, engaged with others in a positive way, is just as important for longevity, according to researchers.

This does not mean you need to go out and join lots of clubs or organizations, that is, unless you really want to. But it does mean you should take some time to think about your social life and the amount of time you spend with other people.

• Make a point to have a conversation with someone every day. This may sound silly, but many people, especially older adults and/or people who are depressed, tend to isolate themselves. When you reach out to others, they will reciprocate.

• Find an organization, club, or group that shares an interest that you have; perhaps a book club, tennis, walking group, poetry writing, senior center, antique cars. Attend a meeting or gathering and meet new people.

• Nurture friendships that you already have. If there are people you cannot physically see because of distance, call and write e-mails often. If they are nearby, get together for tea or a walk.

• Volunteer. This is an excellent way to meet people who share a common interest.

SIMPLIFY YOUR LIFE ONE DAY AT A TIME

Simplicity, simplicity, simplicity

–Henry David Thoreau, Walden

How many times have you said to yourself or heard other people say, "Why does everything have to be so difficult?" "When did everything become so complicated?" How often do you think to yourself, "I wish life were easier?"

Life can be easier. When you eliminate the things that hold you back, bring you down, or throw you off balance physically, emotionally, and spiritually, your life can be simpler. The journey to a simpler life can be one of great discovery, and it can awaken your sense of self and your place in the world. When you shed the things that can weigh you down and distract you from finding your own unique self, you become lighter in mind, body, and spirit. The journey of simplicity begins when you realize that you want change and begin to explore ways to make it happen. This is a time of soul searching, of looking at certain aspects of your life objectively and deciding if they truly contribute to or are detrimental to your life.

Some things to consider:

• Possessions that are no longer meaningful or useful to you. These are items you have stuffed in your garage, attic, closets, storage shed. It is time to let them go. Find an organization, an individual, or a family that can use the items and you will be spreading joy to others as you lighten your load

• Social obligations. If you are attending social or other activities solely to be polite or out of a sense of duty, then it's time to re-evaluate. You could be spending that time doing something more fulfilling.

• Being overbooked. Is every day on your calendar filled in with an appointment? Are all of them really necessary? Are any of them unfulfilling? It is time to learn how to say, "no."

• Doing things because others expect you to do them but that have lost meaning for you. There can be many things in this category. For example, you enjoy the holidays, but you don't want to spend the time, effort, or money decorating the house like you used to. Yet everyone in your family says, "you have to." No, you don't. Is it a tradition for you to cook a huge dinner for certain holidays, and now you don't want to anymore? Then don't.

• End (or significantly curtail) toxic relationships. You know who these people are—they drain you of your energy and your time. You can be polite and yet still firm. They may move in your outer circle (e.g., the sister-in-law who attends family gatherings), but you do not need to allow them into your inner one.

• Eliminate the amount of clutter coming into your space. That may mean stopping the influx of unwanted catalogs and other unwanted mail. For catalogs, you can often call a toll-free number listed in the catalog and ask to be removed from their mailing list. Some companies ask that you send them your mailing label with a note asking to be removed. Not only are you reducing the clutter that comes into your home, you are also reducing waste. You can also go to the Direct Marketing Association's Mail Preference website and make your request for catalogs and mail you do not want to receive.

How else can you simplify your life? Every time you do something that causes you to wonder, "Why am I doing this?" Write it down in your journal. After about a week, look back at the things you listed and think about each one. Is there any way you can change this activity that would make your life easier? For example, perhaps you find that you are running errands several times a day or each week that could be combined if you planned them differently or eliminated some of them. Every unnecessary item, task, and relationship that you can lift from your shoulders makes you lighter. When you make your life less complicated, you can allow yourself more time for joyful contemplation, personal growth, and spiritual development.

REVITALIZE YOURSELF WITH SLEEP

When was the last time you woke up feeling completely rested, refreshed, and revitalized? Was today? Yesterday? Is it many days of your life? If not, you are not alone. Sleep deprivation is one of the most pervasive health problems in the United States. The National Sleep Foundation's Sleep in America 2009 study found that nearly half of Americans surveyed said their sleep needs were not being met, 35% slept less than six hours a night during the week, and 41% have driven while drowsy at least once a month during the past year.

Some people say they are too busy to get the sleep they need, but the truth is a lack of sleep makes you less effective, physically and mentally. So if you think you are getting ahead by not sleeping, you likely are not. Of course, there are many other reasons why people do not get enough sleep: chronic pain, use of certain medications, stress, and sleep disorders are just a few. But because adequate sleep is so critical for overall health, it is essential that you address the issues that are preventing you from getting the sleep you so desperately need. If you are experiencing a lack of adequate sleep, you first need to identify the reason(s) why. If you have a medical condition or are taking medications, talk to a naturopathic healthcare professional about your sleep problems. If stress is a cause (and this is a big one), you need to make stress reduction a part of your daily routine. Several of the tips I talk about in this booklet are a great start. Here are a few more tips on how to get restful, refreshing sleep:

• Practice stress reducing activities before you go to bed, such as yoga, tai chi, meditation, visualization, or stretching exercises.

• Make your sleep environment pleasant: just the right temperature, comfortable sheets and pillows, no distracting lights or sounds. The right mattress can make a huge difference as well.

• Keep your sleeping environment dark. We love the sun, but early morning light can tell your body that it's time to get up when it's not. If there is any light that you cannot eliminate from outside sources, consider wearing an eye mask.

• Establish and keep a regular sleep schedule. Go to bed and get up at approximately the same time on both weekdays and weekends.

• A light snack before bed that contains the amino acid tryptophan and/or a soothing cup of herbal tea can help you sleep.

• Try a cup of herbal tea that contains chamomile, passion flower, valerian, and/or hops. A small portion of nut milk, tofu, or a banana may contribute to your tryptophan requirement and assist with calming your nerves.

• Avoid caffeine and alcohol for at least three to four hours before you go to bed. If possible, avoid them all together.

• Pay attention to the time you awaken at night and notice if there is a pattern. The hours you become agitated or wakeful at night can be indicative of an underlying physical and/or emotional imbalance.

• Turn off the TV. A television gives off light and noise, two things you do not need to fall asleep. If you need some sound in the background, turn on soft, soothing music.

• Avoid sleeping pills. At best they are a temporary fix, and consistent use can lead to side effects and worse insomnia than you had when you started.

Do not ignore your need for restful, rejuvenating sleep. Without it, you cannot live fully in the moment, enjoy all of Nature's creations, and completely interact with others.

CREATE AND MAINTAIN A JOURNAL

Journaling is a private, effective way to explore how you feel about the events in your life. It is not simply a recording of happenings in your life, like a log or day-timer. To be most effective, the process of journaling involves writing in detail about your feelings and thoughts related to the people in your life, stressful events, joyful situations, and the emotional impact they have on you.

Research shows that journaling can be a very effective way to deal with stress, to explore your inner thoughts and emotions, and to problem solve. The physical act of putting thoughts and emotions down on paper has a way of triggering the brain to be more creative and to release emotions that may have been suppressed or unacknowledged. Journaling can open up doors in your heart and mind that help you learn more about yourself and your relationships with others, your work, and your environment. The act of journaling also has been scientifically shown to improve cognitive functioning, strengthen the immune system, counteract the negative effects of stress, and reduce symptoms of asthma, arthritis, fibromyalgia, and other health conditions. You do not need to be a good speller, a grammarian, or a great writer to keep a journal. A journal is your private record, your personal stress management or therapeutic tool, so no one needs to know if you misspell words or cross things out. Journaling is a creative process, a path to self-knowledge, an emotional healer, and a spiritual journey, all on paper. Of course, you can use a computer to keep your journal, but many people find that physically writing is highly therapeutic and relaxing. If your thoughts come too fast to put down on paper, however, you may find that a computer is a better choice for you. If the idea of keeping a journal is appealing, here are a few tips to get you started and keep you going.

• Be consistent. Choose a time to write in your journal. If possible, put down your thoughts every day. If you don't have enough time for writing daily, then choose one or more days and week and stick to it.

• Keep details. When you are writing in your journal, you may think to yourself, "Oh, I'll remember so-and-so's last name, no need to write it down" or "I'll remember that address." Do not assume you will remember details at a later date. Include them at the time of writing your entry.

• Release your feelings. Remember, this is not a log of your life's events, this is an organic, emotive piece of writing. Get beyond facts to include how you feel about things.

• Always date your entries. You may skip a few days or even weeks between entries. Date and even put the time of your entries in your journal.

• Pose questions to yourself. After you write about an event or situation in your life, you may have some trouble assembling your thoughts about it. Physically writing the question, "How do I feel about what so-and-so said to me?" or "How did going to the funeral make me feel?" can trigger your emotions. Perhaps you will not be able to respond immediately, however, if you end your entry with a question you can always come back to it later.

• Do not give up! If you miss a few days or even weeks without writing in your journal, do not be discouraged. Just pick up your pen and begin writing.

STIMULATE YOUR BRAIN

You know you need to keep your body physically fit. What about your brain? Do you exercise it and stimulate it every day? Let's consider for a few moments the wonders of your brain and how important it is to keep learning and expanding your mind.

When you burst into this world, your brain contained about 100 billion neurons (brain cells) that need to communicate with each other all the time throughout your entire life. While you were an infant, billions of these cells formed complex networks that integrated your nervous system, and by age four or five years, your basic cerebral structure was complete.

Throughout your life, your neural networks are in constant motion, reinforcing and reorganizing themselves in response to new stimuli and new learning experiences. Old dogs can learn new tricks. You can and should continue to stimulate your brain and expand your mind every day.

Did you always want to learn how to play an instrument but now you think you're too old? Nonsense! Sure, research indicates that we learn most easily when we are young, however, you can learn new skills and expand on talents when you are older. If you nourish and challenge your brain, you can keep your neural networks operating at an optimal level.

There are scores of ways you can stimulate your brain. Some are so easy, you can do them almost without thinking. Make a point to do something to challenge your brain every day. Here are some suggestions:

•   Change a routine. For example, drive to work on a different route, take the bus to work instead of driving, park the car and walk the last few blocks.

•   Experience a completely new activity. It could be yoga,

tai chi, Latin dancing, painting with wate...
chess, or a musical instrument. You do not need ...
professional—just learn and enjoy.

• Travel. This is a wonderful way to push your brain to absorb new sights, sounds, tastes, smells, and textures. If you can't physically travel, watch travel shows and DVDs. Sure, it's not the same, but you can be an armchair traveler. Get some books from the library on the place(s) you are traveling to, and learn about it as you watch.

• Read. If you love mysteries, great, enjoy them, but also explore other genres. If you would like to share your love of reading with others, you might join a reading group or perhaps become a volunteer reading tutor.

• Play games that stimulate the mind, such as crossword puzzles, anagrams, sudoku, and scrabble.

• Learn a new language. This is one of the more challenging ways to stimulate your brain, yet it can be immensely rewarding. You do not need to become proficient. Just a working knowledge of another language can allow you to perhaps read and translate poetry for pleasure or to write to or speak with someone from a different culture.

... want to be doing in ten years? Five ...morrow? If you have gone through the ...ersonal goals, you probably have the an-...estions. If you don't have the answers, or if you ...... thinking about questions like these but have not yet ta... n the time to formulate some answers, then I would like to help you get started.

The process of setting goals is powerful and healing, and the process of working toward those goals is a journey of discovery and adventure. When you know what you want to achieve, you have a foundation, a basis from which to begin your journey. Having such a basis allows you to focus your efforts and stay on course. It can also give you a great feeling of self-confidence and motivation.

Goals are set on several different levels. First, it is helpful to create your "big picture" goal. This is your grand plan on want to do with your life. You might consider this to be the finished manuscript of your life. Then, as if you were writing the book, you break down your overall goal into smaller ones, the "chapters" of your book, if you will. You can create even smaller or shorter-term goals, like subheadings within the chapters.

This approach to goal setting provides a basis from which to start. Here are some things to think about:

• What would you like to achieve in your lifetime (or perhaps 10 years in the future)? Remember, this is a broad picture, so think about any artistic, educational, spiritual, relationship, career, family, financial, and social goals. Brainstorm your ideas by writing them down in each category.

• When writing down your goals, make them positive statements. For example say, "I will create happiness in my life by becoming healthy in mind, body and spirit. I begin each day with gratitude, prayer, and wheatgrass juice," rather than, "I want to get rid of my cancer".

• Once you have written down items in each category, select one goal in each category that best reflects what you really want.

• Remember, these are your goals, not those of your friends, family, or employer. If you have a partner, you will likely want to consider what he or she wants, however, you should also remain true to yourself.

• Once you have identified your lifetime goals, brainstorm to identify your smaller goals—the ones that you need to finish to reach your lifetime goals.

• You may want to keep a journal of your lifetime and smaller goals. This journal can be separate from your other one. Read your goal journal regularly to remind yourself what you stated that you wanted to do, have, or achieve.

• Create daily to-do lists of things you need to do in order to reach your goals. These will help you keep focused on your goals.

•   Set goals based on performance, not outcome. That is, what action steps do you need to do in order to achieve a particular step in the goal or sub-goal.

•   Review and adjust your to-do lists regularly. Keeping a goal journal will be helpful in keeping track of your progress.

•   Set realistic goals for yourself. That's why it is helpful to routinely re-assess your goals and do some soul searching about how you feel about your goals and your progress.

ENJOY AND EXPLORE YOUR SEXUALITY

Your sexuality is an integral part of your overall health, an expression of who you are, your engagement with the world, and especially other people. While the physical part of sex is important, so are the emotional, spiritual, and mental aspects, because sexual health is holistic.

Sexual expression is the way people show their lovers what and how they feel about them, but it is also an indication of how you feel about yourself. We express our sexuality through words and actions of passion and intimacy, but because these emotions are so powerful, sexuality can be misunderstood, which is why many couples face some challenges during their relationships. These challenges can be embraced and used to help you and your partner come to a better understanding of your feelings, passions, and your own sexuality, regardless of your sexual orientation.

Communication is a key element when it comes to sexuality. Many people know how to communicate about work, current events, their friends and family members, and other topics, but they get laryngitis when it comes to talking about sex and sexuality. Could it be that you have nothing to say? I doubt that, but what you probably need is a little boost of encouragement.

First, you should explore how you feel about your sexuality. Are you comfortable with your sexual orientation? How does having sex make you feel emotionally, mentally, physically, and spiritually? Are you experiencing changes, such as premenopause, pregnancy, or menopause that are affecting how you feel sexually? Do you like your body?

Are you able to ask for what you want from your sexual partner? If you do not have a sexual partner, you should still ask yourself these questions. We are all sexual beings, with or without a sexual partner.

You also need to communicate with your lover. It would help if he or she also conducted an inventory on his or her sexuality before the two of you talk, but that isn't necessary. What is important is that both of you establish an atmosphere of trust, safety, comfort, and love. You should promise to be truthful with each other, and to be kind at the same time. For example, if there is something that your lover does sexually that does not make you feel comfortable, instead of saying, "I hate when you do that," you can say, "I would like to do something new instead of doing that," or "something about this makes me feel a little uncomfortable, so let's talk about it." When you or you and your partner explore your sexuality, remember that it is not something "out there" separate from you. Your mind, body, and spirit are one. To help you and your partner communicate better about your sexual feelings, here are some things you can do.

• Get away for a few hours or a day. It can be a picnic in the park, a walk in the woods, a drive up the coast, a visit to a bed and breakfast, in essence, someplace that is away from the everyday routine.

• Give each other a full body massage with body oils.

• Take a bubble bath together with soothing music and candles.

• Have an indoor picnic.

• Surprise your lover by calling and asking him or her to meet you for a sexual rendezvous.

Exploring your sexuality and that of your partner requires trust, a willingness to be vulnerable, mutual respect, patience, and an ability to pay attention to what your body and emotions are telling you. The results, however, can be enlightening, rewarding, and overall amazing.

VOLUNTEER

We make a living by what we get, we make a life by what we give. –Sir Winston Churchill

The late Dr. Hans Selye, who was best known for his work with stress and its impact on health, noted that when we do something good for other people, we inspire their gratitude and affection, and that this gratitude protects us from the stresses of life.

A woman who volunteers at a hospice unit says that she gets so much love and satisfaction from being with her patients, that she almost feels guilty about feeling so wonderful. It is an example of how love flows both ways in a volunteer situation. That's one of the amazing things about volunteering; although you provide some kind of benefit to other people, an organization, the planet, or some other cause, you get so much in return.

Volunteering can help you:

•   Make a positive difference for people, animals, or the planet.

•   Express gratitude for help you may have received from a group, individual, or organization in the past.

•   Learn new skills and/or polish ones you already have.

•   Make new friends.

- Teach your skills to other people.

- Gain work experience and enhance your resume.

- Build self-esteem and self-confidence.

- Improve your health—remember the stress reduction benefits!

- Serve as a role model for children, to encourage them to volunteer.

If you are interested in volunteering, there are many types of opportunities from which to choose. You might want to help with clerical work in a non-profit office, teach children how to read, visit hospice patients, walk dogs for an animal shelter, or even travel to a foreign country and serve as a volunteer guide, teacher, or environmental worker. Nearly every non-profit organization—large or small, local, national, or international—utilizes volunteers. All you need to do is identify what you would like to do and then find one or more that fit your needs. You might ask yourself:

- Do I want to work with children, adults, animals, the arts, environmental issues?

- How much time can I devote to volunteering?

- What skills would I like to share?

- What skills would I like to learn?

Where should you begin your search? If you already know that you want to, for example, volunteer in a hospital, you can contact those in your area and talk to their human relations department. If you are undecided, contact area non-profits and ask what their needs are. Most cities have a United Way or Volunteer Center which keep lists of volunteer opportunities. There are also many websites that can help you; for example, VolunteerMatch.com, Serve.gov, Idealist.org, and Volunteer.gov, among others.

If you wonder what impact your seemingly small contribution can do to make the world a better place, you would know if you ever spent just ten minutes holding the hand of a person who is in pain or reading to a lonely child. Every act of kindness contributes to the collective consciousness, helping to make the world a better place. You can make a huge difference when you volunteer and help another human being. After all, it is by giving that we truly receive.

PAY ATTENTION TO YOUR DREAMS

Everyone dreams. As we pass through the different stages of the sleep cycle, we go through REM, rapid eye movement sleep, which is where dreaming happens. But many people wonder what their dreams mean; what is the purpose of dreaming? What can our dreams tell us? And how can we use what we learn in our dreams in our daily lives?

I encourage everyone to pay attention to their dreams. You might argue that you can't remember your dreams, or only little bits and pieces that quickly escape your memory. That's okay, you can change that.

The best way to not only remember your dreams, but to establish a relationship with them, is to "get them while they're hot," so to speak. To start the process, keep a pad of paper or a journal and a pencil or pen next to your bed. Then, whenever you wake up, during the night or in the morning, write down everything you can remember. Perhaps all you can recall is feeling like you were falling. Write it down. Or maybe you remember seeing many different colors but didn't know where you were. Write that down. These dream memories may seem insignificant or unrelated at the time you make a note of them, but over time you may likely see a pattern or something that brings many of the dreams together into a cohesive picture or story. Have you ever been dreaming and the dream is so disturbing that you make yourself wake up? The ability to create an intention can be used in another way—intending to remember your dreams.

When you get into bed, concentrate on the fact that you want to remember your dreams that night. Do not make this a stressful event; just keep saying to yourself, to your unconscious mind, that you want to remember your dreams. And you will, perhaps in bits and pieces at the beginning, but remember to write down each and every one of them.

Dreams arise from the unconscious mind, which is part of a greater Collective Unconscious. The way we can tap into what is going on in our unconscious mind is through our dreams. Thus the images that appear in our dreams and the feelings that they invoke are all important because they are telling us something. When you keep a record of those images and feelings, you can put together the pieces and learn what that something is. Some people attempt to understand their own dreams; others seek help from books or individuals who may or may not be trained in dream interpretation. Dreams are highly personal, yet you can get some clues or hints about how to better understand the images and feelings associated with your own dreams by reading about or talking to other people about what they have experienced.

The first step, however, is recording your dreams. I believe you will find the process of noting and studying your dreams a rewarding and enlightening experience, allowing you access to your unconscious and broadening your understanding of yourself and your place in the world.

I also believe that we can program our own dreams by thinking about that which we wish to explore in our dreams. This can add to the fullness of life once we realize that our dream state is really only an extension of reality. It is a way of experiencing more of what we wish to have, create, or do during hours which could otherwise just be "slept away."

LIFE CAN BE SWEET WITHOUT SUGAR

Cookies, candy, cake, chocolate, ice cream, sugary cereals—sweets, sweets, sweet! Americans have a sweet tooth for sugar. The American Heart Association (AHA) estimates that the average American consumes 22 teaspoons of added sugar every day. That is nearly ½ cup of solid sugar, adding up to 355 calories. Each week the average American consumes 2 to 3 pounds of sugar. This is easy to understand once you consider that highly refined sugars in the forms of sucrose (table sugar), dextrose (corn sugar), and high fructose corn syrup are in nearly all processed foods, from bread to breakfast cereals, peanut butter, spaghetti sauce, and microwaveable foods. But all those empty calories are not the only reason why eating sugar must be confined to a minimum.

Many people associate eating too much sugar with cavities and gaining weight, but scientific research shows that sugar can also increase your risk of heart disease, Crohn's disease, gallstones, headache, high cholesterol, gout, and diabetes. Too much sugar has been associated with attention deficit disorder, asthma, mood swings, and kidney damage. Sugar even has a negative impact on your immune system, which means you are much more susceptible to symptoms and diseases caused by invading bacteria, viruses, parasites, and fungi.

For example, one study showed that drinking 24 ounces of cola— which contains about 16 teaspoons of sugar—suppresses the activity of bacteria-fighting blood cells called neutrophils by 50 percent, and that effect lasts for about five hours. How about other foods and beverages? Should you be drinking orange juice for your cold or flu symptoms or eating ice cream to soothe your sore throat? No, not if you want to help your immune system, because both are loaded with sugar. Eating foods high in sugar, fat, and salt makes us eat more foods high in sugar, fat, and salt. These may be our comfort foods or addiction foods and over-consuming them will lead to nutritional imbalance.

So, the secret to breaking the sugar habit is to stop the cycle, which you can do gradually and steadily. Here are some tips:

• Gradually decrease the amount of sugar you eat each day. If you normally drink two cans of sugary soda, for example, drink one, then half, then none per day over a week or two.

• Find other ways to satisfy your sweet tooth. Rather than a soft drink, for example, try seltzer with a splash of natural fruit juice or fresh lemon and mint.

• As you decrease your intake of sugary foods, increase the amount of fresh fruit in season, water, and other food close to their natural state. Feel good about your indulgences of these natural selections.

• Do not substitute artificial sweeteners for sugar, as they will not help you retrain your taste buds. They actually come with their own set of problems discussed later.

- Learn to read labels on foods and choose those that have little or no sugar.

- Learn sugar terminology. All of these are sweeteners: corn syrup, high fructose corn syrup, dextrose, honey, molasses, turbinado, brown sugar, sucrose.

- Will you have cravings? Yes! But you can help satisfy them with a piece of fruit or dried fruit, organic apple sauce or homemade oatmeal cookie.

Life can be so sweet, and healthier, without sugar.

USE NONTOXIC PRODUCTS IN YOUR HOME

Do you consider your home a refuge, a sanctuary, a place of comfort and joy for you and your family? Then it is important to ensure your home is as healthful as possible, and one way to do that is to use products in your home that are non-toxic and environmentally friendly.

Fortunately, there are many bio-degradable, bio-friendly products on the market, and more of them are being developed and introduced all the time. Therefore, if you are not already using such items, it can be easy to make the shift from products that contain toxic chemicals that can harm your health and that of the planet, to those that are better for you and the environment.

In many instances, however, you do not even need to buy specially designed bio-friendly cleaning products, because you can make your own using simple, natural ingredients. The formulas are based on age-old "recipes" that work, they don't harm the planet, and they save you money. To get started, all you need are ingredients such as baking soda, white distilled vinegar, lemon juice, natural liquid soap, and tea tree oil.

For example:

• To make a soft scrubbing solution, mix together ½ cup baking soda with enough natural liquid soap to make a paste. Use the paste on a sponge to wash the bathtub and shower enclosures, counter tops, and other surfaces that can benefit from a soft, nonabrasive scrub.

• To make a window cleaner, combine ¼ to ½ teaspoon liquid soap, 3 tablespoons vinegar, and 2 cups of water. Put into a spray bottle and you're ready to clean your windows.

• To make an all-purpose cleaner, combine ½ teaspoon washing soda, a drop or two or liquid soap, and 2 cups of hot water. Put the mixture into a spray bottle and shake it until the washing soda dissolves. Apply and wipe off with a rag or sponge.

• Do you need to fight mold and mildew? Then try this natural formula: combine 2 teaspoons tea tree oil in 2 cups of water. Put into a spray bottle, shake well, and spray on the affected areas. Do not rinse.

• If you are looking for natural air freshening options,

try lighting a natural candle, burning organic incense, boiling orange peels, spritzing the air with a combination of essential oils (e.g., lavender, orange) and water, or putting cedar chips in bowls around the house.

• If you need to deodorize your carpet, sprinkle baking soda and some dried crushed lavender or basil on the carpet, wait about ½ hour, and then vacuum.

There are many advantages to using natural cleaning products in your home, and especially when you make your own. You provide a healthier environment for you and your family, they are better for the planet, they reduce waste, and they save you money–a complete win-win-win situation!

ESTABLISH A RELATIONSHIP WITH
A HEALTHCARE PROFESSIONAL

Your health is your most valuable asset, and to protect it you need to take full responsibility for your health, your life, and your happiness. One of the most important relationships you can form in your lifetime is one with a healthcare professional. You will entrust this individual with major decisions about your health and your life, so you want to find someone whose expertise, advice, philosophy, and treatment approaches you trust. If you are not happy with your healthcare provider and do not respect and like him or her, this uneasy relationship will have a negative impact on your health care. And that's counter-productive, isn't it? I encourage everyone to take time and do research when looking for a healthcare provider. Naturally, there are occasions when you may need a specialist in an emergency situation and so have to make a quick decision, but in most cases people have some time to do some investigation.

• Get a referral from a trusted family member, friend, or another doctor. This is the best way to find your healthcare partner. Choosing someone from the phone book or randomly from the list offered by your health plan is okay, only when followed up with checking the doctor's reputation.

• Ask the provider how often he or she treats cases that are similar to yours.

• Check on the healthcare provider's credentials and history. The Internet has made it possible to get much of this information online without cost. For information on naturopathic professionals, check the American Association of Naturopathic Physicians. For conventional healthcare providers, there are the Administrators in Medicine, the American Board of Medical Specialties, and the American Medical Association DoctorFinder.

• Visit the healthcare practitioner for a get-acquainted visit. Check to see if he or she gives lectures in the community and/or has a website that you can visit and ask questions and get more information. I believe that a well-informed patient is a much happier, relaxed, and healthier patient. With so much scientific information available on the Internet, patients can research their symptoms or conditions and walk into their doctor's office with a list of questions and (hopefully) a good basic understanding of the issues that concern them. Then patients and their healthcare providers can discuss the matters at hand.

Some healthcare providers are not comfortable with patients who come into their office armed with information and questions. I would advise you to find another provider if this happens to you. You and your practitioner should be partners in your health care, and partners have conversations, not confrontations. Naturopathy is a type of health care that encourages conversation, because it is an approach that is based on the practitioner under¬standing the patient's diet, emotional health, and lifestyle so he or she can work with the patient to assist in restoring balance in the body, mind and soul.

Rather than suppress symptoms, as conventional medicine does, naturopathy addresses the underlying causes of illness and works to bring about homeostasis. Rather than harsh, toxic medications, naturopathy utilizes nutrition, herbal medicine, dietary supplements, acupuncture, homeopathy, body therapies, and counseling to help make life-long, positive improvements. I believe it is critical to establish a trusting, comfortable relationship with a healthcare practitioner who is there for you and your family for everything from the flu to menstrual cramps, nutritional guidance, alternatives to chronic pain management, insomnia, arthritis, and more. A provider who listens to your needs and concerns, who can provide many options for care, and who, most importantly, considers your physical, emotional, mental, and spiritual well-being when working with you to identify treatment options. When you have established such a relationship, you will feel more secure, knowing you have a reliable, trusted healthcare professional you can turn to when you need help.

FORGIVE FREELY

Forgiveness is choosing to love. It is the first skill of self-giving love. –Mahatma Gandhi

It may be one of the hardest things you ever do, and also the most liberating—forgiving someone who has hurt you. When someone you care about wounds you with actions or words, you can choose to bind yourself with negative thoughts or you can choose to embrace forgiveness and free yourself from the bonds of counterproductive feelings. Perhaps your sibling criticized how you raise your children, or your best friend lied to you, or your partner had an affair. These hurtful events can leave you with lasting feelings of anger, resentment, bitterness, and feelings of revenge. When that happens, however, you become a prisoner of these feelings, rather than a person who is free to move beyond the hurts by embracing hope, peace, and gratitude. When we forgive someone, we choose to let go of resentment and thoughts of "getting even." Such negative thoughts can poison your physical, emotional, mental, and spiritual life, and you don't need that! As long as you choose to carry around negative feelings, they will crowd out the positive things in your life, or you will be too anxious, depressed, or angry to even recognize them.

Choosing to forgive is a commitment to make a change, which begins when you recognize that forgiveness is a valuable tool that will allow you to move on once you have wielded it. Then you can think about the situation, your reaction, and how the entire situation has affected your overall well-being. Once you have settled everything in your mind and are ready to stop being the victim and stop allowing negative feelings to control you, you can forgive the person who has hurt you. Forgiving someone allows you to move on and to focus on other, positive aspects of your life. It allows compassion, peace, and kindness to move in where anger and bitterness once lived. However, forgiveness does not mean you deny the other person's responsibility for hurting you, nor does it justify whatever he or she did or said. If your partner cheated on you, you can decide to forgive the person but not excuse the act. What if you can't forgive someone? What if the other person will not admit he or she was wrong or you were hurt physically by a partner and you feel too frightened and angry to forgive that person? If someone has hurt you physically, you may find it extremely difficult to forgive that person. If you are having a hard time forgiving someone, it may help if you write down your feelings in your journal, talk to a spiritual advisor, your naturopathic doctor, or trusted friend. Meditate, or pray. It is important for you to overcome this hurdle because until you do, you will carry the burden of negative feelings with you, and they will weigh you down. Seek help; it is out there, and you will gain a sense of peace. What if you are the person who needs to be forgiven? You could approach the person you have harmed and express your sincere regret and ask for forgiveness. It is best not to make excuses, but to simply take responsibility for your words or actions and admit your errors. You cannot force someone to forgive you, you can only be sincere and wait to see how it plays out.

SPEND TIME WITH ANIMALS

If you have ever had a companion animal or you share your life with one now, I hope every day you experience the joy such a relationship can bring. When you establish a relationship with animals—and especially companion animals such as dogs, cats, birds, and horses, but other animals as well—you expand your connection with the earth, open up new possibilities for communication and learning, and even improve your health. Spending time with animals can be as simple as enjoying the birds that come to your birdbath or the squirrels you feed in the park. But if possible, I suggest you spend more up-close-and-personal time with dogs, cats, horses, even rabbits and guinea pigs.

If you don't have a pet of your own, perhaps you can offer to "pet sit" for a family member, friend, or neighbor, or walk their dog. You could volunteer at an animal sanctuary, animal control facility, dog or cat rescue organization, or other similar animal group in your area. Research shows that spending time with animals can provide you with significant health benefits. Studies have found that:

•   Older people who have pets have better overall physical and mental health than their peers who do not have pets.

•   People who have hypertension and who adopt a dog experience a reduction in blood pressure.

•   A three-year study of more than 5,000 people found that pet owners had lower blood pressure and cholesterol than people who did not have pets.

•   Heart patients who have pets have a much better prognosis than those who do not have pets.

•   Having a pet can relieve loneliness, depression, isolation, and anxiety.

•   Pets encourage exercise and playfulness.

•   Pets satisfy the need for touch and to be touched, and they can provide unconditional affection and warmth.

•   Pets can make us laugh.

•   Loving and caring for a pet can give a person a sense of purpose.

The benefits of having a pet in the home are great for young children. They can develop positive feelings about animals and a good relationship with a pet, which can contribute to their self-esteem and the ability to establish other trusting relationships. Pets can serve as confidants. Young children often talk to their pets, tell them secrets, and private thoughts. Pets can help children learn responsibility by caring for the pet's needs. With a pet, children build a connection with nature and learn respect for other living things. Pets can encourage physical activity, provide comfort, and teach a child about loyalty and affection. Your relationship with animals does not need to be with traditional pets. Some people prefer to spend time with creatures of a "wilder" nature. They may form their relationship at a distance—bird watchers and nature photographers come to mind—or they may get more hands-on experience as a volunteer at a wildlife refuge or sanctuary. I hope you will reach out to the animal world, for it is our world as well. Share time, learn, observe, and grow in your appreciation of life and all it has to offer.

GROW SOMETHING

Plants have the power to heal and to harm, the power to survive and sustain. They can bend the mind and inspire the spirit. –Bernice Walkley Porter

The natural world is rich with plants and animals, and we enhance our lives when we share time and space with these natural creations. I have talked about spending time with animals and in nature. Another way to experience the wonders of non-human life is to grow something. You may already have a garden, house plants, and/or other vegetation that you care for, and I hope you take some time to appreciate their life-enhancing qualities. The idea that gardening and growing plants is therapeutic is not new. Ask anyone who spends time working with plants and you're likely to hear how it helps reduce stress, promotes their creativity, helps them appreciate nature, and improves their overall health. In fact, there is a field known as horticultural therapy, which started in the 1880s. Back then healthcare professionals recognized that working with plants was an effective treatment for people who suffered with mental illness. Since World War II, horticultural therapy has expanded to help people who are experiencing all types of physical, emotional, and mental ailments, ranging from cancer to AIDS, developmental disabilities, Alzheimer's disease, visual problems, and heart disease. Beyond these therapeutic benefits, however, are those that are helpful for everyone: stress reduction, the physical and spiritual connection with nature, and the joy in watching things grow and prosper. If you do not have plants or a garden, you may choose to take some time to enter the world of gardening, even on a very small scale, to experience the connection with the earth and the wonders of watching something grow.

You may want to make your growing projects functional by planting herbs, vegetables, or flowers. A lot of room isn't required to grow these plants. A simple window box with several different herbs can be easy to care for and enjoyable to watch, and you can delight in your harvested "crops" in your favorite dishes. City dwellers who lack a plot of land to call their own can use containers on balconies, front stoops, or hanging baskets in front of windows. Some people who are tight for space and short on windows use grow lights. And then there are community gardens. These are becoming increasingly popular as more and more people who live in urban or suburban areas want to grow their own vegetables but don't have the room and/or want the sense of community that is part of collective gardening. When you participate in a community gardening project, you have opportunities to meet other like-minded people, learn about gardening and share ideas, and develop a sense of pride about growing your own food. Growing plants is also a wonderful learning experience for children. If you have children or grandchildren, get them involved in a project with you and together you can connect with the beauty and wonder of nature through making things grow.

TAKE A CHANCE

One hour of life, crowded to the full with glorious action, and filled with noble risks, is worth whole years of those mean observances of paltry decorum, in which men steal through existence, like sluggish waters through a marsh, without either honor or observation. –Sir Walter Scott

Life is all about taking risks. All of us take hundreds of risks every day—from getting behind the wheel of a car to crossing the street, eating (is the food safe?), mailing a check (could it get lost in the mail?), asking the boss for a raise, even breathing the air (pollutants!). Most of the risks we take have simply become a part of our lives; we have assimilated them into what we do and how we do it. But the risks I'm talking about are different. I'm talking about consciously and deliberately taking a chance, being willing to do something out of the ordinary, something that takes you out of your comfort zone and into territory that is unfamiliar, even a little scary. Such risks can be called leaps of faith, offers you can't refuse, once-in-a-lifetime opportunities, or something not quite so dramatic yet still significant, because they are outside your zone of security. What separates people who are willing to take a chance from those who hold back or who are afraid to put their toe into the water? Fear. Fear of failing, of losing something called security—this feeling of so-called security can be about your job, your home, and your relationships. Security is not something that comes to you from the outside, however. A house, job, relationship, car—none of these things provide security. Security can only come from within you. If you develop inner strength, a spiritual awareness and focus, you will be released from your fears and be secure enough to take chances when the right ones present themselves. Along with the willingness to take a chance, you need to objectively evaluate each opportunity before you take the leap. If you meditate on each opportunity, let in spirit, call upon your inherent beingness, you will know if the risks you are contemplating are ones that you deserve—yes, deserve—to take. You will also know which risks are worthy of your undertaking. All of us are standing on a road that leads to somewhere. For some people it is a road to anywhere; for others, a road to nowhere. Where do you want your road to take you? What are your goals? Your dreams? What are you willing to risk to achieve them? What tools will you use to help you conquer your fears? Are you ready to embrace life to the fullest?

FIND JOY IN YOUR WORK

Do you find joy in your work? How about some satisfaction? Do you like what you do at all? Do you dread going to work every day? Joy and dread are on the opposite ends of the scale when it comes to how you might feel about your job. If you are on the positive side, congratulations! If you can't wait to get to work each morning, great! But if you are drifting toward or wallowing in dread, then it is time to make a change and bring some joy into your work environment. Most adults spend the majority of their waking hours getting ready for, doing, or returning from work. At least part of that time should be joyful, or the stress will continue to wear you down physically, spiritually, emotionally, and mentally. Making a change can mean several things. The most dramatic would be a completely new job. Find new employment that meets your dreams, goals, or desires, and then quit your current job (in that order!). Naturally, this approach does not fit everyone's lifestyle or needs, but if you have set goals and are ready to take a chance, this may be an option for you. Would you like to work for yourself? A recent Gallup Healthways survey of more than 100,000 Americans found that people who run their own business, self-employed store owners, plumbers, and so on, ranked highest in job satisfaction. Psychologists believe this reflects the importance of being free to choose the work that you do, how you do it, how to manage your time, and how to react to problems and adversity. Regardless of whether you choose to run your own yoga studio, bicycle shop, or boutique, having some control over the work and the outcome brings people satisfaction and contentment. (By the way, doctors and lawyers came in second, company and government executives came in third, while farmers and forestry workers came in fourth.) You could also find joy in your current work situation. First, identify what does not bring you satisfaction at work, and then come up with some ways to inject some joyfulness into your work days. For example:

• Are there certain tasks that you do not enjoy or that cause you to feel anxious or stressed? Brainstorm with friends, coworkers, and/or management about what you can do to make this situation better.

• Do you have major disagreements with management or your coworkers? Communication is key. Find a day to discuss your concerns with the appropriate people.

- Are you bored? Brainstorm about ways you can add some new responsibilities or tasks or creativity to your job.

- Another option is to bring or create positive, joyful situations at your work place. You know the old saying, "When the world gives you lemons, make lemonade." Your work place may or may not allow the following suggestions, but it can never hurt to ask!

- Listen to music while you work (with ear plugs).

- Make your work space more pleasant with plants, pictures, or photographs.

- Start an office yoga, meditation, or walking group that meets during lunch. If you can't get anyone to join you, start doing it yourself; others will catch on.

- Start a book exchange or a book or poetry reading group at the office. These can generate stimulating ideas and conversations.

- Smile, laugh a lot, and look for humor as often as possible— and share the laughter.

EXPLORE THE ARTS

Art is a universal language. When you look at a painting, watch a dancer, listen to a piece of music, or touch a piece of sculpture, it does not matter what language you speak or what your country of origin is. The work of art speaks to you, and whatever you see, hear, or feel is unique to you. It does not even matter what the artist intended. If you look at a watercolor of a meadow and you feel sadness and the artist painted it with joy, the fact that the painting evoked emotion is all that matters. You have connected with the art, and the art, with you. If for no other reason, this is why it is important to explore the arts. Whether you actively participate in artistic activities, such as painting, sculpting, dancing, playing an instrument, singing, or writing poetry, or you choose to appreciate the arts as an observer, it is the connection that touches your spirit.

Connecting with art also opens the doors of imagination and creativity. Art triggers the creative part of the brain, the intuitive and spatial part that functions without words and can only express itself non-verbally. Art stimulates the brain by saying, "Here is a box, now think outside of it, change it, and recreate it." Some people think that art is a "waste of time" and need not be taught in the schools. But art is just as important as science, math, and reading, because it is also all of these things. Art helps children understand the concepts of these subjects. Drawing is math, cooking is chemistry, dance is biology and physics. Everyone needs an understanding and appreciation of art to create solutions to problems. Art is what we can turn to in times of inner turmoil and sadness, as well as, times of joy and celebration.

If you already have a relationship with a form of art—say you play an instrument—continue to nurture that relationship, but also explore outside that box into the greater world of music and beyond. Dance and music are a natural combination, but what about music and poetry? Could you write a poem to a favorite musical piece? Do you play a piece of music that invokes certain thoughts and images that you can put down into words?

An appreciation of art doesn't have to cost you anything, or very little at all. Visit an art museum, an outdoor art show; go to the library and bring home an armful of books on art across the ages. You can borrow DVDs from libraries on art, art museums, artists and musicians and their lives, plays, operas, concerts, dance. Make a plan to explore one new form of art each month; say, jazz fusion one month, the Impressionists another month, English poetry in yet another. Who knows what you will discover along the way! You may find out that you are mesmerized by ballet, fascinated by Billy Holiday, can't get enough of Cubism. Your new experiences may prompt you to pick up a brush, tackle a new instrument, begin writing poetry, or get you on the dance floor. Whatever sparks or juices your art experiences set in motion, they will be rewarding, exciting, and enrich your life.

TREAD GENTLY ON THE PLANET

Unless we can preserve places where the endless spiritual needs of man can be fulfilled and nourished, we will destroy our culture and ourselves.

– Sigurd F. Olson, conservationist (1899-1982)

How much better do you think we might treat Mother Earth and all her inhabitants if we regarded her and her inhabitants as our best friends? Would you burn or cut down your friends' houses, use up all their resources, kick them out of their homes and take away or poison their food? I believe it is time for all of us to personalize our relationship with the planet, treat her as a friend, a lover, a child, a parent—someone we love and cherish and would never want to see harmed. When we do, we will tread lightly and gently on the planet, doing what we can to help preserve her beauty and integrity. Every day we hear about the impact of global climate changes and humans' assault on the planet: the melting ice caps and rising sea levels, the plight of the polar bears, worsening natural disasters, the health problems associated with elevated pollutants in the air and water, the vanishing forests, the extinction of species, the burgeoning rise in waste. All of the stories and research and news reports frighten many people—and they should—but not into a state of fear but into one of action. If your child was in pain, wouldn't you help to relieve it? If your friends needed food, wouldn't you help feed them? If your partner became ill, wouldn't you offer comfort?

So it is with our planet. We need to tread gently and lightly, with respect and love. But, you might say, what does it matter if I reduce and recycle, volunteer with an environmental group, use energy-saving appliances, reduce my driving, and eat locally grown food. I'm just one person; how much of a difference can one person make?

Now imagine that there are millions of other people thinking the same thing. And many of those people are going to not only believe that everything they do to help the planet will count; they are also going to be a good friend to the earth because it feels right spiritually and emotionally. They believe that every good effort they put forth has the power to breed and stimulate another good effort, and another, and another.

You have the power to create a better environment. But if you do not let that power out and use it, then it is wasted energy, wasted love. Embrace the world as you embrace a friend or partner or parent. Because the Earth is all those things and more.

ALWAYS GIVE THANKS BEFORE EATING

When eating bamboo sprouts, remember the man who planted them. –Chinese proverb

It is a simple yet spiritual gesture; saying grace or giving thanks before eating a meal. For many people, giving thanks before eating was something they learned during childhood and may or may not have continued as adults. Often, these brief prayers were of gratitude, offered to God or whatever higher power the family held dear to thank the power for providing or making the food available. Today, many people still give thanks before eating, but in some ways the prayers or words of thanks have changed in form, intent, and meaning. For example, more and more individuals realize that the saying "you are what you eat" can have several meanings. When we eat the flesh or other products of an animal, we are consuming the stored memories—including the pain of confinement and terror of slaughter—of those creatures. When we consume plants, we take in their energy memories.

Unless you grow and process all of your own food, you have no control over how it is grown, harvested, preserved, processed, and brought to market. True, you can buy natural, organically grown foods, which I encourage you to do, and you can feel better about exposing you and your family to far fewer toxins. You may also be able to grow your own fruits and vegetables.

But if you are like most people, you depend on the marketplace for the majority of your food. Fortunately, you can cleanse the essence and energy of your food when you offer thanks and blessings over it. There is evidence that prayer can transform the energy vibrations in food and make them more positive, which means the food becomes more wholesome for the body and spirit. A Japanese scientist, Masuru Emoto, has proven scientifically that molecules of water can be affected by our thoughts, feelings, and words. Thus we know that it is possible to energetically improve the quality of our food and water by blessing it. You do not need to stop at blessing the food on your plate. Why not extend your blessings to all the food in the market as you shop? You might send a prayer of thanks out to the farmer in the field as you drive by. Blast a prayer out to the orchards or the fields of wheat or corn. Bestow blessings to the cows and pigs and chickens on the farms, even if you choose not to eat them, for they are creatures on our planet. Remember, to think is to create. When you offer blessings and thanks, you create a higher energy and have a positive impact on the greater consciousness.

CARE FOR YOUR EYES

Eyes are more accurate witnesses than ears.

–Heraclitus of Ephesus (540-480 BC)

The eyes are the windows to your soul and the doorways to your world. They allow you to interact with your environment, and they also can reveal a great deal about your overall health. Despite the obvious importance of eyesight, many people take their vision for granted. That is, until something happens; whether it is an injury, a deterioration in the ability to see, or a diagnosis of an eye condition such as glaucoma, cataracts, or macular degeneration. Keeping "an eye" on your eyesight should be something you do every day, but it is also important to have your vision checked periodically by a professional. One of the best ways to maintain good eyesight is to nourish your eyes with potent antioxidants and other essential nutrients. Several large studies have been done on the effectiveness of various nutrients for the eyes, and the results are encouraging. Not only have scientists identified some very potent antioxidants and phytonutrients (nutrients derived from plants) that help the eyes, these nutrients are found in delicious, natural foods. Whenever you eat these foods, you are helping your vision and your overall health as well.

Here are a few of the nutrients essential for the eyes.

• Bilberry. Studies show that bilberries fortify the blood vessel walls and improve the flow of blood to the vessels that keep the eyes healthy and functioning well. Bilberry also helps prevent macular degeneration and cataracts. Along with eating bilberries, a supplement is available, and a daily dose of 80 to 160 milligrams of the standardized extract is often recommended.

• Vitamin C. This vitamin can help prevent cataracts, delay the onset of macular degeneration, and aid in the treatment of glaucoma. Although orange juice and other citrus are often cited as great sources of vitamin C, many vegetables actually are better, including sweet peppers, kale, collards, turnip greens, broccoli, watercress, and cabbage. Because this vitamin does not stay in the body long, you need to eat plenty of vitamin C rich foods every day.

- Lutein. This phytonutrient is a carotenoid that the body transforms into an antioxidant. Lutein is the main carotenoid found in the center of the retina, called the macula. Therefore it is important to maintain an adequate level of lutein to help preserve the health of the retina. Research shows that 6 milligrams of lutein can reduce the risk of macular degeneration by nearly 57 percent, and the nutrient also greatly reduces the chance of developing cataracts. Lutein is found in red, orange, and yellow fruits and vegetables, such as tomatoes, carrots, squash, and also green leafy vegetables such as spinach and kale.

- Vitamin A. Yes, your mother was right: carrots, which are a rich source of vitamin A, are really good for your eyes. It helps reduce the risk of cataracts. Orange, red, and yellow fruits and vegetables, as well as leafy green vegetables, are good sources of this vitamin.

- Zinc. Did you know that your eyes contain the greatest concentration of zinc in the body? And it is there for a reason: to convert beta-carotene into vitamin A. Healthy sources of zinc include nuts, beans, and whole grains.

- Selenium. This is a trace mineral that has been shown to prevent cataracts and macular degeneration. Studies show that people with cataract often have low levels of selenium. Good sources of selenium include garlic, brewer's yeast, wheat germ, grains, eggs, and fish.

We do love the sun and appreciate its warmth and assistance in creating vitamin D for our health, but we need to protect our eyes from the sun's ultraviolet rays. Sunglasses, either prescription or over-the¬counter, that block at least 95 percent of UV rays are recommended. You might also want to wear a broad-brimmed hat when outside in the sun. Did you know that exercise can help prevent macular degeneration? A study published in the British Journal of Ophthalmology reports that regular exercise can reduce the risk of age-related macular de¬generation by up to 70 percent. Exercise also improves blood circula¬tion throughout the body, including your eyes.

Protect your eyes! They are precious. Said William Blake: "When the doors of perception are cleansed, men will see things as they truly are, infinite."

GET A MASSAGE

Have a heart that never hardens, and a temper that never tires, and a touch that never hurts. –Charles Dickens

For millennia, the Chinese have known and appreciated what Westerners have much more recently come to understand—the healing power of touch. One of the most effective of all the touch therapies is massage.

There are literally dozens of different kinds of massage techniques, but basically their purpose is to bestow some type of physical, emotional, and/or spiritual benefits. It didn't take Western researchers long to discover that massage does more than relieve muscle pain. Studies show that massage can, among other things, help premature infants gain weight, soothe pain from arthritis, boost the immune system, ease symptoms of premenstrual syndrome, lower blood pressure, lessen depression and anxiety, enhance sleep quality, improve concentration, relieve low-back pain, increase range of motion, and relieve migraine pain.

I encourage everyone to enjoy the benefits of a massage whenever possible. Understandably, going to a massage therapist regularly can be costly, but the good news about massage is that you or a trusted partner can learn simple massage techniques that you can do yourself or on each other. Massage techniques can be learned from books, videos, and even online. Massage therapists frequently offer courses in self-massage, and some community centers do as well.

If you have never had a foot massage, you are in for a real treat! At the end of a long day, a foot massage that you can do yourself or have a partner do is an excellent way to relax and help keep your feet healthy. Do you find that your shoulders and arms are tense or uncomfortable after using a keyboard for hours or from driving? A massage of your arms and the tops of your shoulders for about 10 minutes can relax tense muscles and help prevent headache and neck pain. When possible, treat yourself to a professional massage. If you have a massage school in your area, contact them to see if they offer low-cost massage provided by their students. This is a great way to get a massage and help out a student.

As always, the goal is to do no harm. Therefore, you should consult your healthcare practitioner before having a massage if you have certain medical conditions or symptoms. For example, massage may be contraindicated if you have a hernia, osteoporosis, varicose veins, cancer, diabetes, recent surgery, or inflammation. That's not to say that you cannot have some limited massage, say, on your feet. However, it is best to check before agreeing to a massage.

DON'T TAKE YOURSELF SERIOUSLY

Life is too important to be taken seriously. –Oscar Wilde

Don't take yourself so seriously. No one else does.

–Anonymous

Many people have trouble with these two related adages. On the one hand, some may argue, the very fact that life is important is reason enough to take it seriously. After all, people have bills to pay, a family to support, kids that rely on them, nagging health problems, and never enough hours in the day. On top of all that, there are bigger problems to worry about, such as climate change, droughts, nuclear war, pandemics, and fear that someone will try to blow up the next plane they get on. Life just seems to be serious, doesn't it?

Then, what about you? Are you so self-absorbed with your problems that you find it difficult to think about anything else? Are you so afraid of making a mistake that you won't take chances? Have you forgotten how to laugh at yourself— or perhaps you never have. If you haven't, then it's time to learn. Are you afraid others will laugh at you? And what if they do? Their laughter is not a reflection of who you are, but who they are. It can be difficult to not take life and yourself seriously, but I sincerely hope you will shed these burdens. When you take everything too seriously, you miss out on life; you shut the doors to new opportunities, new relationships, and a chance to grow spiritually and emotionally.

Part of life's journey involves making mistakes. I prefer to call them challenges. Perhaps our first big challenge was learning to walk. None of us would be upright today if we had given up the first time we fell when we were learning to walk. If you have a chance, watch toddlers when they are taking their first steps. They plant their little hands and arms, put their butt into the air, and stand up. They totter, they fall, they cry, but they get up. "Failure" and "mistake" are not in their vocabulary. Why is it in yours? We laugh and give encouragement to a child who is learning to walk, but when we grow up, we forget that it's okay to dust off our bottom, get up, and try again. With age, life and how we perceive ourselves and our place in the world, we sometimes take on a serious tone. When we think we have failed at something, we need to re-view the event and accept it as a learning experience. If we can accept the fact that we will not always succeed the first, or second, or even the third time we do something and that these attempts are part of life's learning process, then we have a chance to stop taking our lives and ourselves to seriously. Fall, smile, get up, learn, and laugh. Laughing tends to chase away inhibitions, reduce stress, and trigger a positive attitude. If you are facing a difficult decision or problem and you are stuck, do not beat up on yourself. Shift your attention to something else for a while— something enjoyable—and then when you return to the challenge you can view it with a fresh, more creative and relaxed mind.

Life is so much more enjoyable, rewarding, and exciting when it is approached with a positive eye. I believe that if you practice the pearls I have shared in this booklet, you will realize the joy that lies within you and around you. Can you get "serious" about not taking yourself too seriously?

CREATE SOMETHING

Imagination is the beginning of creation. You imagine what you desire, you will what you imagine and at last you create what you will. –George Bernard Shaw

When you create something—whether you paint a still life, sew a piece of clothing, make a meal, plant a flower garden, or write a poem—you are making a statement and putting a part of your essence into your creation. When you create something, you increase your awareness of yourself and others.

The process of creating can be healing; it can help you cope with stress and relieve pain; it can stimulate your cognitive abilities and enhance your awareness of your surroundings. Creation is a life-affirming process.

You may feel a compelling need to create something. After a disaster or personal tragedy or an emotionally uplifting event, some people experience a strong desire to put their feelings down or get them out in a tangible form. Creating something allows you to do just that. When you are focused on making something, you draw upon internal resources and bring them out where you and others can see and experience them. You attempt to capture what you are feeling and then transform those emotions into the object or whatever else it is that you are producing.

For example, let's say your sister has just announced that she is pregnant, and you are overjoyed for her and her family. You may feel compelled to make a baby blanket or another gift for the baby. Or, a favorite aunt is diagnosed with Alzheimer's disease, and you want to help her so you put together a scrapbook of people, places, and events in her life for her and her family. Or, you are deeply moved by a news report about a dog that has been badly abused in your city, so you write a poem and send it to the local newspaper.

Of course, you don't need a special event to prompt a creative streak. The process of creating something can be a very effective way to cope with everyday stressors. In fact, writing in your journal is a creative act! For some people, being creative means sitting down each day and writing poetry; for others, it may be knitting or sculpting or baking bread or playing music. When you tap into your creative core, you release new energy, stimulate your imagination, and sprout innovative ideas. Once the juices of creativity begin to flow, enjoy the ride of discovery and all the places it takes you.

CHECK-IN AND RELAX

If a man insisted always on being serious, and never allowed himself a bit of fun and relaxation, he would go mad or become unstable without knowing it. –Herodotus (484-430 BC)

Are your shoulders scrunched up toward your ears? Is your jaw tight? Are you tapping your foot or bouncing your leg? Is your stomach tied in a knot? Are you squinting? These are all signs that you are experiencing stress and that you are at odds with your body. These manifestations of tension can cause you to have lingering physical pain and discomfort, as well as have a negative effect on your mood. It's a good idea to check in with yourself on a regular basis—at least once daily—and pull the plug on tension and stress. In other words, relax! Stress has a way of creeping up on us, and before you know it, you are clenching the steering wheel, furrowing your brow, or pacing with impatience. Or perhaps you are a quiet, outwardly passive seeker, who has an internal battle going on in your stomach. No matter how you handle stress, you can turn it around and banish the tension, just about wherever you are.

All you have to do is:

• Check in. Recognize if you are nervous, tense, or stressed, and identify which parts of your body are reacting to the stress.

• Evaluate. What can you do, given where you are at the moment, to alleviate your stress? A full-body stretch may work well at the office but not while you are driving in traffic.

• Whether you are sitting in a board meeting, standing in a long line at the grocery store, mopping the floor, or standing in front of a class of second-graders, you can take a minute or two to relieve stress and then move on with your day.

• Take action. For example, if you are driving in traffic, consciously relax your hunched-up shoulders and take several slow, deep breaths. If you are stopped in traffic, then add gently rotating each shoulder and arm individually. Some teachers involve their entire class in their relaxation breaks by asking the class to stand and stretch along with them.

• Other relaxation tips include: taking a 15-minute nap, listening to music, practicing several yoga poses, meditating, taking a brief brisk walk, doing leg lifts and ankle rotations while sitting. Take time to acknowledge and relieve stress and tension during the day, and you will experience a significant improvement in your overall well-being. You will feel a burst of physical energy, a lightening of mood, and enhanced creativity.

PAMPER YOUR FEET

Forget not that the earth delights to feel your bare feet and the winds long to play with your hair. –Kahil Gibran

Let's face it, you depend on your feet a lot, and it's easy to take them for granted. That is, until they start to hurt, and then you have a challenge on your hands. Because when your feet hurt, it seems like everything is out of kilter. You may begin compensating for the pain, which places stress on other parts of your body. Before you know it, your knees hurt, your hip is throbbing, and you have a back ache. Foot problems often develop from changes in posture caused by carrying too much weight. If you are overweight, your knees may come too close together while you walk, which shifts your body weight to the insides of your feet. This can harm the arches and tendons in the feet and ankle and eventually result in hip and back problems. Do you like high-heeled shoes? Your feet, ankles, and legs are not too fond of them. Shoes with heels affect the natural way you walk. Heels that are three inches put seven times the pressure on the ball of your foot and can damage your bones. Yet the American Podiatric Medical Association says that 39 percent of women wear high heels every day, and 75 percent of them say they have shoe-related foot problems.

Wearing high heels can result in ankle sprains, heel pain, foot deformities, blisters, knee and back problems, and other foot problems.

The best way to dress your feet is with low-heeled or flat shoes that have good arch support. Wear good athletic shoes whenever possible; you can wear them to an event, and then change to your dressy shoes when you arrive! Here are a few other tips to keep your feet happy and healthy:

• Treat yourself and your feet to a foot massage. You can do it yourself, or ask your partner to do it for you. A foot massage is also a great way to relax.

• Use a pumice stone and apply a natural lotion or oil to your feet to keep the skin soft.

• Keep your toenails trimmed. Cut them straight across and not too short.

• Wear shoes that fit. This may sound like a silly tip, but it is not worth it to endure pain or discomfort just because you like the way a certain pair of shoes look if they do not fit properly.

• If you wear socks and stockings, wear ones that fit and change them daily.

• Avoid wearing backless heels because they place undue strain on your muscles.

• Stretch your calf, heel, and foot muscles several times a

day to help them relax and increase range of motion.

• Check your feet often for any cuts, bruises, ingrown toenails, or other problems. This is especially important if you have diabetes or any condition that reduces the feeling in your feet.

• Switch your shoes from day to day. Wear shoes that allow your feet to breathe, especially if your feet tend to sweat. Canvas is an option for people who do not want to wear leather. Sandals are good if they have some arch support.

It pays to be good to your feet, and they will be good to you.

SAY I LOVE YOU OFTEN

I like not only to be loved, but also to be told that I am loved. I am not sure that you are of the same mind. –George Eliot

"I love you." Three simple words, when spoken from the heart, carry an incredibly powerful message. These three words have the ability to change a person's life forever, brighten someone's day, and dissolve feelings of sadness and loneliness. Saying "I love you" to someone lets that individual know that he or she is valued, wanted, and cherished. And don't we all want to feel that way? Every day of life is a gift and an opportunity to let people know how we feel about them. How would you feel if someone you loved died and you had not told him or her how you felt? Never take for granted that someone knows that you love them.

Challenge yourself. How many ways can you think of to say "I love you"? Throughout your day, think about this question, and whenever you think of an answer, write it down. Keep the list in your journal. You may be surprised at how many ways you can name. Think about how you would want someone to tell you that they love you. Imagine you are telling a child, a parent, a partner, a good friend, a sibling, a grandparent. Suddenly the list of possibilities grows!

Because actions speak louder than words, you can also say "I love you" with a touch, your eyes, a smile, a gesture, a token. A flower left on someone's chair, a note tucked into their book, writing someone a love poem, suggesting a walk in the moonlight; these non-verbal ways to express love are just as important as uttering the words and they can complement the words as well.

Every day presents an opportunity to share your feelings with those you love. When you extend your love to others, you get back so much more than your give. Let the people who matter the most to you know how you feel. Say, "I love you." Say it often, and say it with your heart. Every time you do, the good feelings join the collective consciousness and help make it an even more powerful, loving, and creative force.

CLEAN YOUR INTERNAL HOUSE

A man too busy to take care of his health is like a mechanic too busy to take care of his tools. – Spanish proverb

Do you treat yourself and your house to spring and fall cleaning sprees? Do you enjoy how it feels when the house is aired out and everything smells fresh and clean? When we clear out the dust and clutter from our living space, it can feel like the house emits new energy and vitality, ready to face the environment once again.

That's how your internal house can feel after you have completed a detoxification. No matter how much you try to eat the right foods, drink pure water, and keep your home and work space toxin free, the world constantly exposes you to contaminants that can invade and build up in your body and have a negative impact on your physical, emotional, mental, and spiritual health. That's when it's time to do a little internal house cleaning. Do you feel sluggish or out of synch; are you experiencing skin problems, aches and pains, headaches, fatigue, or digestive discomfort? An internal house cleaning in the form of a detoxification can rest, clean, and nourish your body and restore internal balance and health.

Before you attempt any detoxification program, you should talk to a healthcare provider who is knowledgeable about such plans. A naturopath is your best choice. He or she can help you identify which type of detoxification program is best for you and your lifestyle. Make sure you tell your healthcare provider about any medical conditions you may have. If you have diabetes, for example, or take medications, your detox program will need to be specially designed to take these factors into consideration.

A detox program can help your body by:

• Stimulating the liver to eliminate toxins from the body.

• Prompting the elimination of toxins through the skin, intestinal tract, and lungs.

• Improving blood circulation.

• Nourishing the body with healthy nutrients.

• Allowing the organs to rest through fasting.

A detoxification program does not need to be extensive to be effective. Although many detoxification programs are for seven days, you can do a shorter one, based on your needs and lifestyle. One simple detox program involves drinking only fresh fruit and vegetable juices and water for three to seven days. To enhance the elimination of toxins, a detox program should also include light exercise (e.g., yoga, stretching), dry-skin brushing, deep breathing exercises, herbal and nutritional supplements, and hydrotherapy (e.g., sauna). Herbs that help cleanse and protect the liver include dandelion root, burdock, and milk thistle. Green tea is a rich source of antioxidants and should be a part of any detox program.

Always remember though, that supplements must be properly selected to match your body's physiology and particular constitution. There is not one detox protocol that will suit every person's needs. Herbs each have their own mechanism of action in the body and must be selected and administered properly and in a correct order which will allow their maximum effectiveness.

Naturopathic physicians are the only licensed professionals who have been trained for four or more years in the proper usage and administering of medicinal herbs. Also, it is important to know that all herbs are not created equally. The quality and quantity of active ingredient in the correct ratio and combination with other substances or physiological factors is relevant. Please do check in with your Naturopathic physician before starting any protocol designed to detoxify or heal your body.

Completing a detoxification program properly can restore your energy, vitality, and overall well-being and make you feel like you have "cleaned your house thoroughly."

In Closing . . .

So there you have it. Was that fun, interesting and insightful? I sincerely hope so. As I said at the beginning of my book, I had the opportunity to learn all of this wisdom through my own personal experiences. Like any parent who wants to advise their children wisely so that they don't make the same mistakes that they made or have to suffer unnecessarily. I present this work… the pearls of wisdom from over 20 years of clinical practice, plus the most important life lessons I have learned. My goal is to gently guide and remind you of what your mother may not have told you. My mother did not have the opportunity to advise me and so I have taken on the role of mother, and loving, caring, yet firm, doctor.

There are so many other Wisdom of Well-being lessons for us to explore: how to prevent and reverse PMS, how to transform into the second half of life gracefully, preventing osteoporosis and decline of hormonal vitality, action steps on how to create and maintain a positive attitude, healthy preparation for pregnancy and pearls of wisdom for new mothers, as well as, necessary guidelines for teens for the prevention of acne, eating and stress disorders, and books for children, so that they may learn while they are young, (and so that they may remind us of course) what is imperative for excellent foundational health. Please look for these editions throughout the rest of the year.

Our magnificent creator created us perfectly and in harmony with nature. An important difference and distinguishing factor between us and God, is that we humans have the ability to make choices. Our purpose as spiritual beings is to evolve the soul to a higher level and work through the temptations and lure of the physical.

Let's all rise to the occasion, becoming our healthiest and most vibrant selves, so that our contribution to this universe will be meaningful and fulfilling. Please listen to your body, pay attention to your intuition, and BE SMART... Your health is in your hands.

To be continued...

Thank you so much for being in my Life.

With Love and Aloha,

Dr. Diana Joy Ostroff may be reached at:

The Center for Natural Healing

5283 Kimokeo Street

Honolulu, Hawaii 96821

tel: 808-373-9966

fax: 808-373-3456

Please visit our website at: **www.naturalhealinghawaii.com**

Additional credits:

Deborah Mitchell, Editor

Bonnie Lee Chappell, BLCGraphics.com, Design

Richard Baccigaluppi, Visions of Paradise, Photos

Made in the USA
Columbia, SC
12 January 2020